TO GOD BE THE GLORY

Regina Mixon

Affordable Publishing
PO Box 720952
San Diego, Califorina 92172

(866) 661-8821

TO GOD BE THE GLORY

All Rights Reserved

ISBN: 0-9778348-5-9

Published by:
Affordable Publishing
PO Box 720952
San Diego, CA 92172
Toll Free: 1-866-661-8821
www.shabach.org (click) Affordable Publishing

No part of this publication may be reproduced, stored in a retrieval system, or transmitted in any way by any means – electronic, mechanical, photocopy, recording, or otherwise, without the prior permission of the copyright holder, except as provided by USA copyright law.

Printed in the United States of America

Contents

Forward.. W Terrell Snead, II, Pastor
The Word of God Missionary Baptist Church Los Angeles, CA...IV

Credits...V
Dedication..IX
Introduction..X

Chapter One.. 1
The Beginning

Chapter Two.. 11
The First Wedding Date

Chapter Three..22
The Second Wedding Date "The Day I Married the Lord"

Chapter Four...27
The Waiting Period—Introduction

The Waiting Period/The Breaking Period 32

Chapter Five..122
The Big Day

Chapter Six...138
God's Store House

Chapter Seven...153
And Then There Was Glory
Prayer for Salvation and Deliverance...............................181

"To God be The Glory" The title says it all, because only God can be glorified for the healing and deliverance He gives to His children. As you prepare to read this book, prepare your hearts to receive the healing and deliverance God has ordained for you.

Jesus said in Luke 22:31-32, "Simon, Simon, Satan has asked to sift you as wheat. But I have prayed for you Simon that your faith may not fail. And when you have turned back, strengthen your brothers." (NIV)

This book is a classic example of that passage of scripture. This woman of God allows us to peek into her personal life and share the struggles that many are facing but are ashamed to admit. God has turned her misery into her ministry and revealed the purpose in her pain. So I encourage you now to prepare your hearts to be blessed and get ready to walk in the newness of life.

Pastor W. Terrell Snead, II
The Word of God B.C. Los Angles, CA

Credits

    Credits are given throughout this entire book to many people. Special thanks goes to the City of Minden in its entirety and surrounding churches; Pastor Rodney, Evangelist Cynthia Williams and the King Solomon Baptist Church for having faith in me and the vision God had given me; Creflo Dollar, my spiritual father for a long time; Drs. I. V. & Bridget Hilliard, the ones God led me to pester the most; the Trinity Broadcasting Network and its affiliated churches and pastors; Christian Worship Center in Alexandria, Louisiana; Bishop T.D. Jakes and his beautiful wife, Serita; Prophetess Juanita Bynum Weeks; Joyce Meyers (my spiritual mother for a while); Bishop Paul and Co-Pastor Debra Morton; John Hagee Ministries; H.O.P.E (Homeless Organizations Providing Empowerment); Service Connection; Feed The Children for providing us with food boxes to feed those in need; L.A.N.O (Louisiana Association for Non-Profit Organizations); Bonnie Moore and Lane Richardson with Centerpoint; Bishop Noel Jones & The City of Refuge. Last but not least, my Pastor, Rev. W. Terrell Snead, II., Pastor of the Word of God Missionary Baptist Church in Los Angeles, California. Pastor, without you and your faith in God and me, none of this could have happened. I thank you so much.

    Special thanks also goes to Mrs. Frankie Mitchell, the one person other than my grandmother and aunt who has influenced my life at an early age. It is because of your belief in me that I dared to dream. You always said that we could do whatever we wanted, and to never let anyone tell us otherwise. You were, and still are a great teacher, both in and out of school. I love you so much, and you know it.

    I could not go a step further without acknowledging my aunt, who is a cross between my big sister, my mother, and my best friend. Without you none of this would have been possible. So, Bertha Mitchell, I give thanks to God every day for giving you to me. Paw Paw (Willie James Bradford), that goes for you as well.

I give thanks to God for all of my family members… Bruce, Della, Dwayne, Phyllis, Kelvin, Dorothy, Jeffery, Dee Dee, DI, Rickie, Cliff, Gene, Kinedia, Shimetre, Linzo, Trish, Leroy, Janet, Byron, Sophia, Annette Jefferson, Annette Jones Davidson and Women of Purpose & Determination, Sandra Wafer, Georgia (Bonnie) Kirts, Mack, Willie T., Mattye Lane, Gloria Alstork, Debra Miller-Mills and yes, even, Curtis ☺, Charlotte and Ed Williams, Danny & Jennifer McKinney, Minister Mary Colquitt and so many others.

I would be remiss if I failed to include the ones who contributed the most during this entire period and who sacrificed the most…my children, Kendrick, Nikki, my daughter-in-law, Keisha and my godchildren, April Brown-Sterling and Shiemetre Brown-Smith. They contributed so much and made so many sacrifices I cannot even begin to thank them for all they have done.

My children were very instrumental as they were my helpers, my sounding boards, my partners and my gifts from God. They were there for me and even though we fussed, we always seemed to pull together.

I would also like to acknowledge a mighty woman of God. She has done to me what I have done to many others. I am thankful for her pushing me in the right direction when I veered off course, got tired, or just wanted to give up….Mrs. Gail Marie Hughes King. Thanks so much. I don't know if I could have even finished this book without you. You played the role of my counselor, my comforter, my boss, my friend, and you played each role well. Thank you so much. I still think you're strange. ☺

Special thanks are also extended to Barbara Haynes, Sue McClendon, Linda Kinchelow, Deborah Banks and Terry McNulty. I have been blessed by God to have true friends in each of you. Thank you all.

I dare not forget my play niece, Evangelist Shanta Goodrum. This girl pestered me often. When ever I prayed and asked God for help, she would always show up. It got to a point when I had to be more specific in my prayers. It did no good, she still came. She said it was like "The Preacher's Wife", where the preacher prayed for help and Denzel showed up often then later the preacher didn't want him. She was right. Thanks Evangelist Goodrum.

Special thanks go to Mr. Jeff Brown who had enough faith in me to rehire me after I quit working for the the Social Security Administration for over four years. It's because of you that I found the strength to fight my way back to go forward. You took a giant leap of faith in hiring me again. There is absolutely no way I could have done it without you. Thank you so much.

Thank you to my ex-husband, Anthony Arline, a great and mighty man of God. You kept me laughing, crying, and you were such an encourager. We will be family until death do us part.

This book would never have come into fruition without the help of my Publishers at Affordable Publishing. Dr. Carroll and all the others who helped in any way to make this happen, I say, "Thank you" **and** we do have a lifelong partnership. Thanks for your prayers, words of encouragement, numerous emails, proofing, proofing, and more proofing. Thanks to each and every one of you for everything.

Thanks to the makers of the movies "Pretty Woman", "The Best Man", and "Soul Food". Thanks to Mel Gibson and all those involved in the makings of "The Passion of the Christ"; to Tommy Tenney for "One Night with the King"; to Bishop T. D. Jakes for "Woman Thou Art Loosed" and all of the other teachings he's done.

And last, but definitely not least, I give thanks to God for Rev. Robert James White. This man endured so much throughout the course of these writings that I know he is a mighty man of God.

When you read, you will understand why I say this. Thank you so much for everything.

And finally, *"TO GOD BE THE GLORY!!!"* for the things He has done. I just thank God for all. If your name is not included, know this, I thank God for each of you as well.

Dedication

This book is dedicated to the memory of my grandmother, Mrs. Emily Wilson Richardson. My grandmother was a mighty woman of God, a praying grandmother who instilled in us at an early age the morals and values of life. She probably thought that we had all let her down. "Mama, we want you to know that your prayers and works were not in vain. You taught us what family was, and still is all about. For that we can never repay you. We let you and ourselves down many times but, ***"TO GOD BE THE GLORY!!!"*** we finally got it right. We know the angels of heaven are rejoicing with you today. We have never, ever in our lives been poor but always rich in what matters most—God and family. We have always been very much blessed. It may have taken us, or rather some of us, a little while to realize it but nevertheless we are blessed.

We learned from you that a family can and should pray together, work together, play together, learn together and prosper in life together. We learned through many mistakes that God and family are what matters most in life. United we can win in every area of our lives…all of us.

We pay homage to you today for being that praying mother and grandmother and we thank God often for having blessed us with you. We are spreading the legacy with our young so that they can continue spreading it as the years go by and each of us comes to join you.

We love you, we always will, and we will forever keep your memory alive!"

With love,
Gale

Introduction

As you read this book, you will be moved to laugh, cry, be shocked at the ridicule received by "religious people", amazed at the number of people who attend church on a regular basis, and who doubt the written Word of God.

You will experience a range of emotions. My initial reaction was anger. I was so surprised by the disbelief…shocked is a better word. Still, it did throw me for a loop for a minute.

My brother, who I often thought was totally insane, had realized early on that God **is**. I now know that he is a great man of faith. I am now just as strange as he is…maybe a bit more strange, but guess what? "But ye are a chosen generation, a royal priesthood, a holy nation, a *"Peculiar"* people; that ye should show forth the praises of him who hath called you out of darkness into his marvelous light." (I Peter 2:9)

In this book you will see that God is a God of miracles and as the scripture states, "With Him nothing is impossible" (Luke 1:37). I pray that you are strengthened in your walk with the Lord by reading this and *Know* that if, and when, God gives you a vision, the only one who can stop it from coming to pass is *You*!!!

When He impregnates you with something, rest assured that if you have faith as a grain of mustard seed and you put some works with your faith, it **shall** be done. *__Not it may be,__* but it ***shall be*** and it will *__all__* be done for ***His glory***. "TO GOD BE THE GLORY"

XII

CHAPTER ONE
The Beginning

When starting the final writing of this book, I asked God, "Where do I begin?" His response to me was to start at the beginning. Wow! I thought this is going to be extremely hard as by starting at the beginning it gives an in-depth look into my life. Talk about skeletons coming out of the closet.

So, in obedience to Him, I start at the beginning. The story that is shown in this book is nothing but the truth. "And you shall know the truth and the truth shall make you free." (John 8:32). The purpose of this book is to set many free; to let all its readers know that with God nothing is impossible, no matter where we started, or where we find ourselves now or how many mistakes we've made in our lives.

Okay, so we go to the beginning of my story. I was born and raised in a small city in Louisiana, the third of six children. My beginnings were not so uncommon for many born in my home town. Our family was dysfunctional, my father was an alcoholic, my mother drank and so many cover-ups took place.

I know this may be upsetting; however, the story has to be told. So I go on…I don't remember much of my childhood years. It seems the only pleasant memories I have are those when I along with my siblings, lived with my grandmother. My grandmother was a praying woman, a woman after God's own heart. The memories in her house were those of meals being cooked, three times a day. Not from boxes but home cooked meals.

There are memories of fruits and candies smelling up the house during the holidays. Memories of her humming while cooking a meal. Sometimes while humming, tears were streaming down her eyes. Tears of sadness many times as well as tears of joy at other times.

At Mama's house, the freezer was always full. She, along with some of us kids, picked peas, shucked corn, made preserves, baked breads, pies and cakes. The most important thing she ever did was provide us with endless amounts of love, instilling the values of family and telling us how we were special. We were poor by the world's definition but rich by God's definition. We were rich in what mattered most. Those were the good times.

Mama passed away when I was nineteen years old and much took place from childhood until that time. Even more happened afterwards. I wish I could say it was more positive things but that was not the case.

As I mentioned earlier, I was born into a dysfunctional situation. I actually still do not know what a functional home is, but nevertheless, I strive to know. I remember at an early age how my father had taken me to a *juke joint* and in front of many drunken men told me how he was not my father. He asked me several times to tell them who my Daddy was. Each time I responded "you" he would say "no, I'm not. Tell them who your father is." Talk about being hurt. I could not have been any more than three or four years old but the picture is etched in my mind and heart and will probably be there forever.

He has since departed this place and I forgave him a long, time ago. We actually became very good friends some years before he died. It took a bad situation to bring us to that point. It happened nevertheless. That's what matters.

My mother (referred to as Madea) was a good woman. I sometimes believe she drank as a means of escape from the situation at home. I could very well be wrong but I do believe this. She made sure our clothes were always ironed and kept my hair pressed and together at all times. She was a beautiful woman in my eyes.

My mother died when I was eleven years old. I've always

believed the real cause of death was a broken heart. Two of the six children born to her had died; one after childbirth and another lived a few months. To me, she was a queen. She always let me know that I was loved. She also informed me early on as to who my real father was.

Shortly after my mother died an older male cousin started to come around quite often. He seemed nice at first. Soon after I learned that his looks were deceiving. He asked me to baby-sit his children while he and his wife worked. Seeing an opportunity to make some money, and after asking my grandmother for permission, I said, "yes". That "yes" led to molestation later. He was the first man who had sex with me and it hurt terribly. I remember him going off to work, his wife leaving the house, and him returning back home earlier than he should have. Those were the worst nights I have ever experienced. I thought I would die.

This continued for a long time, actually for many years. I tried in every way I knew how to tell my grandmother without actually uttering the words. He tried to convince me that he loved me and it was a normal thing for people to do when they loved another person. I felt like dirt. When I went to school I didn't feel that I fit in. That was the beginning of a downward spiral into promiscuity, alcohol, and drugs as an escape.

After him and a couple of other men, I became pregnant at the age of fifteen. I had a beautiful daughter but was not ready for motherhood. My daughter was born perfect in every way, but later was diagnosed with a serious illness. A little over age one she was in a vegetable-like state and could no longer do anything. She later had to be placed in a State School and subsequently died in October 1985.

I remember one day I sat her on the car to take her picture. Another lady was supposed to have held her. She fell from the car. I've carried the guilt feeling as though I was to blame for her becoming disabled for years.

I'll never forget the night the phone call came. A few of my classmates and I were sitting down having dinner at one of our classmate's house. I cried and cried and of course, I felt worthless. I buried my daughter.

At age sixteen, I met a man with money, a powerful figure in our city who also ended up being someone who physically abused me anytime he liked and as often as he wanted. At first I thought I deserved it, then years later I realized no woman deserved that kind of treatment. He, like my relative, said he loved me. Love hurts. I can remember one time he took me to a cemetery and told me he was going to kill me and leave me there with the dead. I can remember jumping from the back of a moving truck and running like crazy towards home because I just knew that time would be the time he would actually kill me. I can remember going to work with black eyes and busted lips many times. Boy, can I remember. I also remember many times having a gun put down my throat and told if I blinked or said anything he would kill me. Abuse in one way or another had become a part of my life, especially from the men who supposedly loved me.

By age nineteen, my mother and grandmother were gone. I felt so alone even though I was not. I have an aunt who has been absolutely great all of my life. She has tried to help me in any and every way possible for as long as I can remember, but the kind of help I needed she could not provide. I sought that help through alcohol and drugs and men and more men. I was looking for love in all the wrong places.

After my grandmother died, I ended up living with and caring for my two younger brothers and my older brother. God had blessed me with a good job working for the government and I was able, or so I thought, to take care of them. I really was not. I was a mess!

My younger brother entered Job Corps, which was a good move for him. My middle brother and I have always been extremely close. He has been like my left hand all of my life. I made his life a mess. How could I help it? Mine was a mess.

During all of this time, the one thing I continued to do was to go to church. We were brought up in the church and in Mama's house going to church was not an option, you had to go. This is why I continued to go. I know I was hoping to find some kind of relief there. I went hung over. I went after being beat up. I went with thoughts in my head of partying afterwards. I went and I even sang in the choir. Yes, you heard me right. No matter what church I was in or what state of mind I was in, I sang for God. I believe I was actually crying out to God.

People looked at me most of the time because I tithed, I am a giver by nature, and because I dressed well. They would continually say to me, "You are so good, God is going to bless you". I was screaming on the inside, just begging for someone to feel my pain and help me, later realizing that no human being could.

Let me stress at this point, this book is not a gloom, despair and agony story. It is one that shows that even though things don't happen in our lives as we think they should, what the devil means for bad, God often turns into good. This is a story of hope and encouragement; one that states no matter where you are in life, you are not alone. God loves you and He is the lover of your soul. He alone can do what no man can and God often takes our miseries and turns them into ministries.

Later on, God blessed me with a wonderful son. It was because of him that my life started taking a few positive changes ever so slowly but changes in the right direction nevertheless. I wanted to be a good mother. I wanted to love him and let him know how special he was. I wanted to shield him from the harms of the world. I wanted him to know that he could do anything he desired if he really wanted to and I continually told him this over and over again.

This is not my biological child nor is it my adopted child. He is my God given child. His mother, because of her problems at the time, found she was unable to care for him and allowed me the opportunity to do so. Was I really qualified to raise a child with my life being such a mess? In a word, "no". Did it stop me? No.

I was blessed with him from three months on. He is now twenty six years old. He was, and still is, my gift from God. I loved him as best as I could, but I made a lot of mistakes.

My daughter came along in June of 1987 and at that point I knew my life needed to change even more. I vowed that nothing like I had gone through would ever happen to her. I made a promise to God and myself. So, what did I do? I married her dad about a year after she was born. I just knew with us raising her together, she, as well as my son, would be brought up the right way and he could provide the protection. Wrong again.

Did I go to God in prayer about my decision? No, I did not. Did the marriage last? No, it did not. He was a good man but he was not a Christian. I'd better say I don't believe he was. He worked and was a good provider, initially. Soon drugs came on the scene and that marriage was over. I went through the usual with him, things that go along with crack addiction, the stealing of money and belongings, taking the car and being gone for days, things like that. I kept thinking I could help him and maybe I could save him. I couldn't even save myself.

Okay, so marriage number one is over. The children did not really understand what was going on and neither did I. I thought that the *"until death do you part"* stuff was real. How could my first marriage end in divorce? "What therefore God hath joined together, let not man put asunder". Did God join us together?

Before I could bounce back from marriage number one, I am in a mourning period and I find myself looking again for love in all the wrong places. What stupid thing do I do now? I meet another good man who was a smooth talker. I wondered, what do I do? You answered correct. I got married again.

Now you might ask, "Why does she keep getting married?" Good question. I'm glad you asked it. I got married both times because all I heard from the pulpit was, "Shacking up is a sin." and "If you're going to fornicate you'd better get married and do it right". I did what I believed to be right, after all, I had a history of sexual sins and now I was trying to get it right.

Guess what happened folks? The second husband was also addicted to crack cocaine. Another great man and after God finishes with him; I believe he will really be on fire for Him. That doesn't change the fact that he was not ready for a marriage. Heck, he could not even take care of himself. I saw all of the signs but again thought I could change him. Wrong again.

This man was such a smooth talker and so wonderful that after divorcing him, I turned right back around and married him again. Was I nuts? Yes!!!

I thought my first husband took me through the wringer. What he did was nothing compared to what the second one did. He took everything that wasn't nailed down. I slept with my purse underneath my pillow most nights. He would take the car and disappear for a week or two at a time. Many times while I was walking to work or getting a taxi for my kids to get to and from school, I would see others driving my car. He would actually rent it out to folks!

By the time he would come home I would be too angry to fuss or fight; too hurt to talk and just too glad to finally get my car back to do anything. He would have periods where he was off the stuff. Those periods didn't last long. It was during those times he went to church, threw away his drug paraphernalia and we walked together in one accord. It never lasted long enough to really enjoy it.

Finally, I divorced him the second and final time. Enough was just enough. Seeing my kids look at me with pain and hurt in their eyes and always remembering the vow I had made caused so much hurt and pain inside. I could have just crawled in a hole and died. But I didn't. I kept going on. I kept going to church. I kept singing in the choir and I kept praying. I believed somewhere deep inside of me that there really was a God and I just knew if I kept crying out to Him eventually He would hear my cries and He did.

I came to realize much later that God had been working in my life all along. I did not actually come to this realization until about eight years ago. It was at that time that I felt a "calling', so to speak, on my life. I did not know exactly what the calling was but knew within my spirit that there was something that God wanted me to do. I thought for the longest time it was to sing praises to Him and I was perfectly content in doing just that. Was I mistaken?

In 1996 I felt a strong urging within to quit my job and go to Bible College. At that time, I submitted my letter of resignation and then told others of my plans. You can imagine the negativity that cropped up after telling others. You see, in the city that I worked in I earned in excess of twenty dollars per hour. To some of the people there, that was the equivalent of being rich. They could not even begin to understand my thought of quitting such a good job. I withdrew my letter of resignation and continued working at my good government job. The more I worked, the more dissatisfied I became.

From 1996 until the latter part of 1998, I went through pure hell. I was a tither, a giver, yet my finances were a mess and I could not for the life of me understand why. I had always heard, "Give and it shall be given unto you" and "The more you give, the more you would receive" so I gave. I looked for so many ways to give. I never expected anything really in return. I just love to give. So why were my finances such a mess? I'll answer that...God has a way of giving and receiving and it is spelled out in His word. With my life being out of order; disobedience to the word taking place, I was not reaping the rewards of being a King's child. There had to be a breaking. I did many things not because of disobedience but because I was naive to many things. "My people are destroyed for lack of knowledge…" (Hosea 4:6) You see during this time I thought I was doing, for the most part, what was right. Partial obedience is disobedience.

On September 21, 1998 I had surgery. The doctor placed me on bed rest for six weeks. At that time I thought that I lost my mind. I literally started to lose my mind but I started to get more of His. It was during this time that I first heard and knew the voice of the Lord. When He spoke to me I nearly fell out of the bed. I thought "what in the world is happening to me?" and "who's talking to me?" From that point on, I was never without a constant companion.

Being new to hearing from God, what did I do? I blabbed it to anyone and everyone who would listen. Did they think I was totally insane? Yes, they did. I heard comments like, "I know God speaks to people but He does not speak to them every day." or "She's just thinking that stuff herself". The best one and heard most often was "She has lost her mind". I realized years later I just could not tell everyone what God was saying to me. By the time I realized it the damage had already been done and I was a marked woman.

Being new to hearing from God, for a long time I did not realize that Satan speaks to us as well. I later came to recognize when God was speaking and when the enemy was trying to imitate Him. "My sheep hear my voice, and I know them, and they follow me." (John 10:27)

I said to God after the laughing and ugly comments, "God, you've got me acting strange and the people think I'm crazy". His response to me was "Who cares?" I am breaking you down to build you up." And the breaking began. God also told me that He was going to allow Satan to touch my life and it would hurt, but rest assured in the end He would get the last laugh. He assured me it was well. It was, and is.

You will read of my three wedding dates in this book. The second wedding date was the day I married the Lord; dressed in a wedding gown in the church, I announced to the small number of people, "On this day I had married the Lord". Crazy wasn't even the word. Insane was much more appropriate or so they thought.

One of my girlfriends said to me after the ceremony, "You are living the book, *The Lady, Her Lover and Her Lord*" by T.D. Jakes." and being more specific she pointed out the section in the book entitled, "Her Lord". What was so ironic was the fact that I had the book, but never actually read it. Each time I went to specific parts of the book and I did realize that particular section was in direct correlation with where I was in my life. Awesome!

Now that your curiosity has been peaked, we move on to the next chapter. We'll get into the meat and potatoes of the story now that some background information has been provided. You will not believe the following chapters, or maybe you will. It was hard for me for a long time but here we go…

CHAPTER TWO
The First Wedding Date

September 21, 1998 started off as any other day. The only difference was that this particular day I had surgery and was scheduled to be off work for six weeks. The surgery was nothing major, but major enough to warrant time off to properly heal.

During those six weeks, I spent about two of them actually in bed. After that, I worked around the house like a mad woman. I cleaned closets and cleaned the entire house from top to bottom. I did laundry…washing, ironing and putting away. I hung curtains and moved furniture. Folks around me could not understand why I was doing all of this when I was supposed to be on bed rest. Neither could I.

The doctor had told me to not do any heavy lifting for six months. Well, I said he should have been very specific to my higher power as it was He who led me to do many bizarre things.

It was also during this time that an inner voice continually led me to file for divorce. I eventually did and it was the first of many legal documents to follow. I can remember being at a girlfriend's house and making mention of my intent to file for the divorce. I said to her that I knew I needed to do it but I just didn't have the time. Her response was, "You're off work. You know how to do the papers. I have a word processor and you say you don't have the time. You're going to pay someone to do it when you can do it yourself; that's real smart. What's the problem?" Needless to say, she was exactly right. I filed for divorce for the second time from my second husband. This led to the beginning of my assisting many others in helping to file legal papers or rather simple legal documents. I was not practicing law, by any means, but rather sharing the new found information learned. That will be covered later.

October 26, 1998 was the day I will never forget. That was the actual day the Lord first spoke to me and I knew it was Him. Well, I didn't at first. I was lying in bed and I heard His voice so clearly say, "With your mouth you are willing and obedient, but you are also like a little kid who has been told to clean your room". He continued to say, "You are pouting and not doing what I, the Lord has said for you to do. I have told you to do some specific things and you have not done them yet". I almost fell out of my bed. I thought, "Am I losing my mind?"

A few nights before then I was lying in bed and all of these questions came to mind for me to ask someone I had just recently met. Questions like, "What do you like to do for enjoyment?" and "Why are you in the ministry?" I had actually met this person in August of 1998 and was not even interested in knowing the answers to these questions yet they kept coming to mind. Actually, I was trying to sleep and I could not go to sleep without first writing those questions down. Well, something inside *told* me to ask this new friend of mine those questions. I thought, "What am I going to do with the answers?" and "Why do I even want to know? I am not even interested in knowing these things". I placed them aside and went on about my business.

I thought, this man will surely think I'm crazy if I ask him these questions. They were nothing bad…just things like, "Why are you in the ministry?", "What do you do for fun?", and "What are your goals, visions and dreams?" Questions like that. I'm actually interviewing this man and for what? Don't get me wrong, he was nice enough. Actually he seemed to be a very nice person. I just wasn't interested in him in a way that these questions implied...

I eventually asked the questions. He seemed to be so excited to answer them and he did so, one by one. Okay, so what am I supposed to do with this new found information? Get ready for this, God is telling me that this man is the husband He has planned for me and that he is His best choice for me. Right!!! After all, I've always known what was best for me and this man sure was not. He was nothing like the men I was accustomed to, which actually was a good thing. I asked God, "Are you sure he's the one?" God answered "Yes". Okay.

After the question and answer session took place, I went on. After all folks, I'm really not interested. I attended a Women's Conference and heard Bishop Debra Morton speak. Her message was "Is It Your Turn or Your Time?" That was my first time hearing her speak and it was dynamic. This was a weekend long event and the second day of the conference was the first time I heard John P. Kee's, "Turn Around". It was a life-changing weekend.

Nothing else memorable happens until November 3, 1998. It was at that time that this voice within me led me to go and buy a name plate for this man…you know the one. I bought it and then had an inscription placed on the back of it. What did it say? "From your wife". This was to be his wedding gift. Ha!

Later that month, I heard that it was time to plan my wedding. So you know I did. I bought a ring…a man's wedding band. I actually bought it later. I was gone! Literally!

It was at this time that God spoke to me and told me that my latter years would be the best years of my life. He said to me, "For all of the sufferings that you have endured, I will now show you My rewards". He continued to say, "The husband I have for you will love you more than you have ever been loved before in my life". That sounded pretty good to me.

By this time, I was in love with an invisible man and a voice. I wrote out my wedding announcement. Detailed to the *"T"*. People, what was missing? If I am doing all of this, where is the man? Does this man have a family? I don't know, nor do I care, because God said I was going to get married and that was enough for me. Was I even seeing this man or dating him? No way. It was settled.

After the surgery and up until that time, I had been losing weight like crazy. Of course, if you're moving everything that's not nailed down and cleaning like crazy, you're bound to lose weight.

The Holy Spirit spoke to me one day as I was cleaning and said "You already have your wedding dress". I said "Where?" and looked up on the top shelf of the closet and there was the dress I had bought when I married my first husband. I said "Oh, no, I'm not getting married in that dress. I married my first husband in that dress". I had the dress cleaned and boxed. God said to me "You're right. You married your first and second husband. I had nothing to do with those, but I am putting this one together". "Whoa!" I said, "Knock me down and call me stupid".

The Lord went on to tell me that He had been supernaturally taking the weight off of me so that I could fit into that dress. Did that dress fit and did I look good the day I married the Lord? Double "Yes"!!! You *darn tootin'* it fit and I looked good. But that's another chapter. I want to add, not only did He take the weight in the form of extra pounds off of me, He also took weight of caring for others from me. You'll read about it later.

I am so gone now. I get on the phone and call up several girlfriends and I tell them I'm getting married. I called up the one who introduced me to my new friend first. After all, she had to know. She didn't say much, just asked who I was marrying and when I told her, I believe there was silence or maybe she said "get real". I can't remember the exact words but she thought I was out to lunch.

Do I stop after that phone call? No, I don't. I call up everybody. I'm telling folks I'm getting married. I tell anyone and everyone who will listen. Many congratulated me…at first. Some of these same people thought later that I had lost my mind and did not hesitate to express it.

It was during this time that I developed a hunger and a thirst for the Word. I stayed up half the night watching Trinity Broadcasting Network; reading different books; reading the Bible and/or listening to tapes of different ministers. Joyce Meyer, Creflo Dollar, Bishop T. D. Jakes, Bishop Clarence McClendon, Eddie Long, Prophetess Juanita Bynum and so many others were my means of getting the spiritual food I needed. During this time, I didn't just see or hear them, I actually started keeping journals of their messages and buying book after book. Reading has always been a love of mine but definitely not writing.

It was also at this time that God kept telling me to get my house in order. I thought He meant cleaning it up, so I cleaned and cleaned and cleaned some more.

If that wasn't enough, after getting my house spotlessly clean, I started going to others houses cleaning. I've always taken great pride in being a neat person…neat dresser, neat in my house, neat all the way around. I could not for the life of me understand why "getting my house in order" was so important. Those of you that are Christians know that it was not even about the physical dwelling. The house He was referring to was my life as a whole.

I have always liked an immaculate house. I have always liked to have everything in its proper place. Cooking was never my forte but cleaning was. I told my children throughout their childhood years that the house had to stay clean as they never knew who I might bring home from work with me or who might drop in. I sometimes went overboard with it. Don't laugh at my ignorance. You might have benefited from it. If I cleaned your house, you did. Those that I didn't help, oh well.

A girlfriend of mine did come by and assist me in properly doing wall-groupings during this time as well as how to use flowers to decorate. By putting our talents together, the house went from being just a clean house, to a well balanced, beautiful home on the inside. Color schemes were developed, things matched and blended well.

My daughter, poor thing, just sat and watched. She had no clue as to what was going on. How could I explain it to her? I didn't understand much of what was happening.

So, we go back to my preparation for my wedding. If I had not been so far gone, I would have realized that no wedding was actually going to take place. People, I did not have a man. How could one take place without the main ingredient?

I did so many weird things…like cutting up credit cards, checks and any other cards I owned. God said I was a new creature. I was really sold out. I would bounce checks thinking a lot of the times that I had enough money in the account to cover them. Balancing a checkbook was unheard of. Some things were better left alone. Why take the time to write down ATM transactions? I would just be asking for trouble by doing that, so I didn't. Why did I want to take a real hard look at my finances? I already knew it was a mess. Of course, this kind of stuff was costing me an arm and a leg but I just didn't want to face the truth. Not yet anyway.

Now, the Lord starts telling me during this time that He is breaking me to build me up. Why do I need breaking? I'm okay. On the fifth of December of 1998, God told me that he had given me the gift of prophecy, it was new to me and I would have to learn how to distinguish when He is talking and when Satan is talking. He also told me when in doubt, pray in the Spirit.

Later in that month as I was preparing to go to church, I was sitting in the family room at about six thirty that morning; suddenly I lifted my hands and started praying in tongues. God let me know that I was interceding in prayer for Pops. I knew in my spirit that something had to have happened to him or something was wrong. I stopped praying at around 6:44 a.m. and was in perfect peace. Later that morning, I heard sirens and instinctively said, "That's Pops". By the time I got to church, the call came saying that Pops was in the hospital.

I wasn't surprised at all.

Leaving church, I went to the hospital. On the way there, the Holy Spirit spoke and said for me and my sister-in-law to lay hands on him and pray for him. When I got there, she wasn't there. Pacing the floor, I waited. She came. We prayed. Afterwards I left to visit my son. I knew Pops would be fine.

That same morning was the first time I heard the song, "The Lady, Her Lover & Her Lord", [Jakes, T.D., Sacred Love Songs (1997)]. I was on my way to visit my son who was incarcerated in Monroe. I pulled off the road to call my sister-in-law and tell her how awesome it was. I didn't get her, but I immediately fell in love with the song. I said "That's me." God said, "That's not only you, but many". Awesome!

After visiting with my son, I made the drive back home. The trip was about an hour and fifteen minutes so I started speaking to God and listening to Him. It was at this time that He said to me that I was pregnant. You can imagine my shock as I was well past forty then and unable to bear children. I asked Him, "How?" Every question I asked in reference to this, the answer was always the same. "I'm a God of miracles". "And her name shall be called Glory which is the highest praise".

Later I realized that when he said I would be, or rather was already pregnant, it was not a child He was referring to but rather a ministry.

December seventh, God gives me the song "The Lady, Her Lover & Her Lord" as the processional and says that I will sing "To God Be the Glory" as a salute to Him and my husband. Yes, we're back to the wedding now.

I searched high and low for that song. I just knew I had it there somewhere. Found it…Vickie Winan's CD has a beautiful rendition of the song as well as the words on the label.

I'm at it again. I contacted a DJ at a record shop and had him record me a tape of wedding songs. He gave me the song "A Love like This" by Phil and Brenda Nichols and told me how hard it is to find that one now. He said it's almost impossible. With God, nothing is impossible.

God told me that same day that the husband He had for me did not know that He was doing this. I'm so sure he didn't. I know he didn't.

That evening a revival started at my church and visiting preachers from all around were speaking each night. It was raining cats and dogs. I toyed with the idea of not going but a male friend of mine, who had problems with drugs, just insisted on going. I thought, God is really up to something and must want to bless him, so I went. I just knew that God was going to do something miraculous for him. I don't know whether He did it for him, but for me— most definitely.

Earlier that day, one of my girlfriends had given a plant to my sister-in-law. I had wanted that plant really bad as it was beautiful. A plain and overflowing ivy. I needed that plant. The preacher, after finishing the message, said that God had him do something that day that he had never done before. He said that God had him cut his baby (as he referred to it), and that someone in the church wanted it real bad; someone of great faith. I'm sitting in the back of the church (which is something I normally never do), and all of a sudden when he asks, who wants it, my hand shoots up. All I could think of is how badly I had wanted that plant earlier in the day. In my mind, I could hear "that plant is for you. You know how you asked earlier for a plant, well this one's for you". I went up and got the plant and that night was the very first night I was slain in the spirit and the second time speaking in tongues.

Before this had happened to me personally, I thought that people just fell out and it wasn't real. I came to know that night how real it was. The preacher prophesied over me and confirmed some things that God had already spoken in my life. He told me whatever

I did to not let that plant die. He went on to say for me to keep in touch as my life would never be the same again and that God was going to raise me up. He was so right but not after breaking me down first. "To every thing there is a season, and a time to every purpose under heaven...a time to break down, and a time to build up". (Ecclesiastes 3:1, 2)

From this point on, I continually hear the voice of God speaking to me. I also continue planning for a wedding. The key word here is "I". There's still no man.

I read the book, *How to Be Led by the Holy Spirit*, by Hagin, Kenneth, then went to sleep. I had the strangest dream. In this dream, my daughter opens a door for a man and lets him into the house while I slept. My eyes were blinded. It was like they were glued shut and I was unable to see who the person was. The more I told him that I could not see him and did not recognize him, the angrier he became. He was so angry that he was about to attack me and suddenly, Jesus appeared on the scene. He took the attacker away and as He did, He said, "I'm taking this demon to the very pits of hell". He was smiling as He said it and as they descended. They both started out adult size and then shrunk and went under the sofa. It was as if it was on instant replay as that scene repeated at least three times.

Then, in the same dream, a girlfriend was quoting the words from Bishop T. D. Jakes, (The Lady, Her Lover, and Her Lord)..."who would have thought with all the pain you've gone through and who would have guessed". Then later, she says, "they thought she'd lost her mind". Those are not the Bishop's exact words; nevertheless she was saying them in his voice. Strange, huh?

This particular friend, by the way, was also experiencing some really strange things taking place in her life. People thought we both were nuts.

I had visions...open visions of my life to come. I saw my husband and I ministering together. God promised me a life of happiness for all the pain I had experienced. "Declaring the end from the beginning and from ancient times the things that are not yet done…yea, I have spoken it, I will also bring it to pass; I have purposed it, I will also do it." (Isaiah 46:10, 11)

Just to let you know, while I'm planning this wedding the divorce has taken place between my second husband and I already, so I'm not totally insane. Well, maybe just a little.

I get my gear together. Yes, you heard me right…my gear. I pull down my husband's gift, my shoes, earrings, pearl beads, garter, and the works. You know in all of my planning, I had a wedding announcement typed and ready to go. Well, it didn't get sent. You can probably guess why.

I'm still cleaning like crazy, staying up all hours of the night. Cleaning, ironing, and watering plants…I worked. It was at this time that God reminded me that when my wedding takes place, it would be a time of sorrow as well as a time of rejoicing. I couldn't deal with that. I was already seeing and hearing too many things.

By the way, the date I repeatedly heard was December nineteenth. It's the eighteenth now and do I have a husband or has anyone proposed to me? No sir. Well, God told me I would get married on that date and I wanted to do as He had instructed me so I continue to prepare.

We're on the day that this grand event is to take place. I called the judge and got a verbal okay to get married without a license and waiver of the three day requirement. He was about to go off somewhere for the weekend and said he'd sign the necessary papers the following Monday.

Finally, it dawns on me that I am not even about to get married. Oh, well. Did I get my signals crossed somewhere? Was it God doing the talking?

To conclude this chapter, I can say that I actually ended up enjoying this day or what was left of it. I put on my wedding dress. It was a bit too tight still then. The jewelry matched perfectly. I placed the veil on my head. In my eyes, I looked absolutely stunning. I will not be defeated though, so even though it didn't happen this time, I'm waiting for my husband. After all, God promised it and He is not a man that He should lie.

CHAPTER THREE
The Second Wedding Day
"The Day I Married the Lord"

    The day after my wedding was *supposed* to take place, I went to church. The service was wonderful; the Holy Spirit was sweeping through the place. The choir is always slamming for the Lord and today was no exception. Christmas dinner was served at the church, so we continued to fellowship after the services were over.

    The following day I felt the need to write my friend a letter explaining some things. This letter was the first of many hundreds of others to follow. Yes, you heard me right—hundreds. Anyway, I explain that even though he didn't marry me, just how blessed I am. I informed him that I had been filled with the Holy Spirit and basically told him how great I was. The letter went on to say how God was doing all of these wild things in my life, and if he wanted to blame anyone for my bizarre behavior, blame God.

    Tonight, I hurt deeply. I asked my daughter if she could get one thing for Christmas, what it would be. She said, "Momma, I told God if I get nothing else for Christmas, all I want is for you to stop smoking." How can you not love a daughter like that? So unselfish… I pray God grants her request. I don't have the willpower alone to do it, so He has to help me. I no longer enjoy smoking. It's a filthy habit that I hate I ever picked up. "God, hear our prayers, please".

    After the Healing & Deliverance Revival, I stopped smoking for four days. I was delivered. When that wedding didn't take place, I started back. I was trying to figure out how I got the messages crossed and used them as a crutch.

    Christmas comes and I give this man the name plate with the inscription. He was so shocked and confused. He called me at my girlfriend's house and said he didn't understand it. I knew then he had not read the letters sent him. So, what did I do? I took him more to read.

While reading the Bible; I stumbled upon the scriptures referring to how God had shown the Israelites the Promised Land. (Exodus) Because of their wondering, they wandered for forty years. I thought, "I'm not going to do this. I'll do it right this time". So, in my doing it right, I write this man and tell him he has one last chance to ask me to marry him. I was serious.

I fast and prayed; praying for my marriage, my children, my church, my family, anybody and everybody who comes to mind. Later, while visiting a girlfriend, I told her that I had received a message from God. I shared with her how I believed I messed things up due to my actions. I kept wondering why, for the longest time, I could not even tell him about the wedding. After all, he's a man of God. He should believe this, right? Sometimes, I would hear a voice that would say, "Tell him" and then other times I'd hear a voice that said, "Don't tell him". I never could figure that out.

I'm searching for answers now. I search the Word. I search in other books written by men and women of God. I am off searching. No one believes me now. That doesn't stop me though.

On the 28th of December, God revealed to me that it was His plan for the wedding to take place on the 19th, but because of my disobedience, it didn't happen. He led me several times to tell my friend what he was saying. I did not know at the time that it was Him. You're probably wondering by now, if it was Him, why didn't it happen. Glad you asked. His time is not our time and His days are not our days.

So, I say to God, "If you're speaking this to me, surely You must be doing the same with him". I kept saying to God that this man would think I was crazy. Reality check. He did a long while ago. I said nothing to him, but I told anyone and everyone else. What did I tell them? I'm getting married. That's what.

Somewhere along the way, *I get* a second wedding date. This new date was Saturday, January 16, 1999 at 2:00 p.m. I said, "I'll get it right now", and I told him.

The Lord revealed to me that my friend had another car and it was at his mother's house. He also gave me another list of questions to ask him. Here we go again. Can I just be normal now, God? Can we just forget all of this stuff? I don't know why you keep telling me this about this person as I don't really care for him in that way. Can we please just move on?

This time there were only four questions. That was good. This time I had no plans of asking those questions either. Well, maybe after we were married. What would I do with these answers? I did ask him about the car and he told me that he did have another car at his mothers' house. Neither he nor God told me what kind it was. I guess I didn't need to know.

January 3, 1999, a few days before the wedding, God gives me a ring size. He told me my future husband's mother would wear a size eighteen dress size. I then proceed with writing yet another letter. This one tells him how the past two and a half months, all I continually hear in my spirit on a daily basis, is his name. It's always something pertaining to him. I tell him how God has been preparing me for him. I also tell him that God has shown me that at the same time this wedding takes place, I will lose someone very close to me; someone I love dearly. I go on to say that I would much rather keep the people I have and love already than have any husband. However, God shows me I can't play let's make a deal. I conclude with how it's not my plan but rather God's and He'll reveal it to Him, if He hasn't already.

God spoke to me and said while He was dealing with me, He did not want any interference. He said he did not want me to listen to anyone except Him now, that He was training and preparing me.

After receiving the second wedding date, I got into action again. I had a fellow co-worker do the programs. I ordered the cakes. I called the pastor. I ordered the flowers and even called around and got the men's sizes to order tuxedos. I was a busy bee.

I prepared the menu. I took care of everything. You might think after "I" did so much the first time, why did I believe that this wedding was going to take place. Anytime one has as many "*I's*" in something, there is definitely something wrong. Was God planning this wedding? Yes, He was. He was planning my wedding to Him. Before I could unite with anyone His way, I first had to be totally sold out and married to Him. Too bad I learned this much later. Let me rephrase that, I learned what it meant to be sold out or married to Him later.

I contact someone and have them in place to do the video taping of the ceremony. Flowers were ordered from someone I had just met and delivered on the day of the wedding. I did not pay her or the video person one cent that day. I did pay them later, though. When the flowers came and everything else was in motion, I just knew that this man would show up. He said he had no reason to show up. He didn't. I just didn't realize it. That day was not about him.

I and my girls, decked out, marched up to that church, an hour and a half late. I could not walk down that aisle without being completely dressed. I wore the wedding gown, veil, garter, everything and announced to the meager crowd gathered there that "today, I got married. I married the Lord".

Afterwards, I went home and broke down. I cried like a baby for a few minutes. It didn't last long, as there were too many prayer warriors there. They embraced me and we prayed. We went on to have a really good time. A statement was made that, "God just showed you that he wasn't the man you thought he was". Someone else agreed. How could he not be the man I thought he was? I didn't think he was any kind of man. I'm confused.

We're sitting in my bedroom and I hear, "It's not over." I thought, surely this has to be the devil. I couldn't sit still after that. I got up and started cleaning and dusting, trying to do anything to ignore that voice within. Another girlfriend of mine came and spoke the exact words I was hearing in my spirit. I blew up and called her Satan. More specifically, I said, "In the name of Jesus, Satan you have to leave". I didn't mean for her to leave, I just knew it wasn't God speaking. She was hurt and left.

When I went to her house, she told me that I had upset her so that she had written me a note. Small, couldn't even begin to describe how I felt that day. I apologized profusely. She loves me and she forgave me. Thank God. She's a good friend.

To summarize this chapter, this time I really did get married… I married the Lord. I'm sold out. The best is yet to come. You think this is bizarre, keep reading. You haven't seen anything yet.

CHAPTER FOUR
The Waiting Period
Introduction

    This particular chapter is the longest one in this book. It covers the period of years that I experienced *all* of the emotions mentioned earlier. It was also during this time that God allowed Satan to really touch my life and it hurt tremendously.

    Events are told merely for the sake of hopefully making believers out of nonbelievers. This breaking took place among my family members and in my own home. What better place for God to break one than in their own home? After all, when God is preparing one for ministry, we have to get bold enough to say "God said" to those in our families first. After that, it's no problem to go any where and say "God said". It's always the ones closest to you that are the hardest. So, again I say, this is not to smear anyone or ruin anyone or in anyway paint a negative picture. These are just the facts.

    You will read some daily notes about many ridiculous things that took place. You will read as to how God was moving in my life and how He used others to help break me. I really did not know just how messed up my life was.

    In this chapter you will see that through it all, I was like a tree, planted firmly. No one could sway me from what God had spoken or shown me. No one, no matter what they said, did, nor how many times they tried. I shall not be moved. God said the stuff. I believe it and it's settled. Well, almost. There were some times I doubted. Those times were not too often, yet there were those times.

    Many times, I begged, pleaded, prayed, cried, and did basically some of everything to get God to release me from this…whatever this was. It surely did not seem like any kind of a blessing but rather curses. Finally I realized this was not just about a man or rather a husband. This was about ***His*** glory. This was about my getting my life in order to minister to other hurting people and to receive the blessings He had for me. Even though, I said many times that I was ready. I really wasn't until much later.

    I fought with God until I'd get just plumb tired. Exhausted! I was fighting a losing battle. When He has something for a person to do, they ***will*** do it. He doesn't force His will on any, but He knows just how to whip us to get us in line with His will for our lives. I got a beating.

    Since God had shown me that it was His will for me to have a husband. He showed me repeatedly that He was not going to allow me to go higher without one. So, I set off to help Him. Especially since the one in my dreams was so darn uncooperative. Most of the time we could not stand each other—literally. He took great pride in reminding me how he did not want a relationship with me, not now, not ever. That was fine by me. I can always get a man.

    Somewhere along the way, I fooled around and fell in love with this man for real and I knew I was in trouble. I tried hard to fight it, but I couldn't. Well, not until later. You want to hear something funny? During this period which consisted of many years, I met and fell in love with, at least three men. All of them are great men of God. They're just men with problems. When He finishes with them though, they will all be great. I came to realize during this time that God does not only give us one choice but ***choices***. I also came to realize that God will bless us with whoever we choose if that relationship is in line with His word.

    It was during this time that I learned to keep my mouth shut. You know I learned this lesson after opening it about a hundred times too many. What God speaks is usually for my ears only ("Oops…open my mouth, insert my foot!"). People do think you're strange when you're telling them what God is saying to you about your own life, their life and others. I've come to the conclusion I'll forever be strange. I'm okay with that now.

God told me when I tell people things He's shown or told me in reference to their lives; it is like I'm opening their mail before they read it. I said, "Well, don't show me, please".

This was a time of learning—lessons about friendship (be careful who you call a friend), lessons about money management His way, lessons regarding conducting business, lessons from the Bible on how a Godly woman should be…just a time of lessons all the way around; my role as a help meet. Say what? It took me a long time to learn these.

The importance of helping those in need was a valuable lesson learned. This was learned by His allowing me to walk through the needs and feel the pains of many. That was the one that hurt the most.

Every one of my family members thought I had lost it and we all fell out with each other from time to time during this period. Estranged from my family, my church, my friends, my job, my every thing, I came to know and rely on a power so much greater than any of these. I came to know **Him**!!!

During this time in my life (from 1999 to the present), I came to realize just how important family is. Family, even though they don't understand, will usually come in when the rest of the world turns their back on you. Family can, and should be many in our lives. A family consists of every born-again believer and is not necessarily limited to those in our blood lines. Natural families, church family, work family…so many others. I've got a huge family and a great one it is. We keep increasing daily.

My children are my gifts from God and they are the best that anyone could ever ask for. Yes, they have their problems and so do I, but they are my gifts. There were many times they thought I had "wigged out". They still loved me and know beyond a shadow of a doubt that I love them. I reminded them of this often. They still didn't understand for a long time.

Coming to realize that God can love you in a way that no human being can was the greatest of the lessons learned. At our weakest moments, He will come in and massage our hearts and minister to our spirit like no human can. He's awesome and so real!

I got out and met people within the neighborhood that I had not actually taken the time to chat with before. It wasn't that I had any preconceived ideas about these people. It was just that I ran around so, I didn't take the time to get to know them. You never really know someone until you meet and talk with them. There is some good in the worst of us. So many have gifts buried inside of them. Stir up the gifts. Use them for His glory.

Everyone faces a storm or many in their lives. We must have compassion and encourage people when they're going through whatever they may be going through. Be kind to people. You don't know what that person is going through, why they are where they are, or what challenges they face. My grandmother always said, "The same people you meet going up, you will meet coming down, so treat everybody right". The Bible says it this way, "Be not forgetful to entertain strangers: for thereby some have entertained angels unaware". (Hebrews 13:2) You never know who you're talking to. Always remember the golden rule…do unto others as you would have done unto you.

Empathize with people in their going through. Maybe you cannot relate, but we are not to judge and we can show mercy After all, it is only by His grace and mercy that we are where we are and we still aren't all that. "Wherefore, let him that thinks he standeth take heed lest he fall". (I Corinthians 10:12) "If we say we have no sin, we deceive ourselves and the truth is not in us". (I John 1:8)

God gave us a commandment to go into the entire world, teaching all nations. (Matthew 28:20) If you haven't walked in their shoes, you definitely don't know what they're going through. Uplift, encourage and tell that person about God and His goodness. After all, we're supposed to be about kingdom building. Those that are whole have no need of a physician. Jesus said he came to seek and to save that which was lost. Let's get about His business.

Christians should not be whining, sniveling cowards but rather strong and courageous. Even when we are weak, we can tap into the source to give us the strength to go a bit further. The joy of the Lord is our strength.

Put God first in all that we do…our time, our talents, and our all. It's His rightful place. Shower His love on all you meet so that all may one day see His face. Never forget where you have been and never look down on others. That addict, wino, prostitute whatever, just might be your sister or brother.

These are the lessons I have learned and I gladly share them with you. Maybe you won't have to go through what I did to learn them. Be not only hearers of the Word but doers (paraphrased James 1:22). Being stubborn and hardheaded like I was gets you nowhere.

Now, we proceed to the dated entries. There were just entirely too many to capture in this book. Don't laugh at me as you just might see yourself somewhere later in the writings. Some of these will make you laugh yourself silly. Others will bring tears to your eyes. As I went back and reread the material, I thought, "Did I do that?" Yep, that was me, so read on…

THE WAITING PERIOD
The Breaking Period

    Well, I really could not for the life of me figure out where I went wrong. After all, God said the first time around that the marriage didn't take place because I didn't tell him. Him being the man I am supposed to marry.

    Okay, so it's January 23, 1999 and God gives me yet another speech. It went like this, "This wedding has been planned for three different dates. Not by Robert and myself but rather by God and me. On January 16th, I married the Lord. This time I am marrying my lover....When will He come through? He comes through every time!!!"

    There is no indication that any type of wedding is taking place at any time in the immediate future, BUT you know I am totally gone now. When? I still don't have a clue. I just know that it's coming because God said it.

    March 19th rolls around and in my spirit I hear, "Robert is taking you to Mississippi." and then "Robert is coming." and "Robert is not coming". By this time, I have gotten totally fed up with hearing anything from anyone in reference to Robert. You know by now the only one saying anything to me was God and Satan. Need to add at this point that I met so many *"Robert's"* over the years I actually got sick when anyone came near me named Robert. My dentist, mechanic, and the person I bought furniture from, the real estate agent, my girl friends husbands, my sister's cousin, the car salesman, a young man who attends our church, Robert with the Credit Union and the photographer. It seemed that no male entered my life and actually did anything for me except men named Robert. Well, there was one, but we'll get to that later.

Hearing things like "Nikki will open the door for him.", "You'll be there when the letter gets there", "Allow Me to bring it to you.", "Monday is not too late." and "It started with '***DI***' and it ends with '***DI***', had me completely baffled.

As I would hear these things, questions would arise within me. Questions like "When?", "What letter?", "Bring what to me?", "Which Monday?", "Not too late for what?", and "What started with DI and ends with DI?" Needless to say I got no answers to any of these until later and I mean much later.

God said to me that it was time for me to announce my calling to the ministry, quit the job with the Social Security Administration and request a dismissal of the Chapter 13 I was under. Whew! This is just a bit too much for me. Leave my comfort zones!!! Is this God?

The strangest thing happened on March 21st, 1999. Standing in the kitchen window I began to hear in my spirit all of these things I would say in church. He told me that I would testify as to His goodness. I thought, boy the Pastor is really going to give me a long time to testify. It was at that point God said "These are the words to your first message". Say what??? Nearly passing out, I said to the Lord, "God you're going to have everybody laughing at me". His response, "there are too many preachers in the pulpit now that are not telling of my goodness. Satan is real but I have ***all*** power and I am ready, willing and able to bless my people. Tell of My goodness." I'll tell it and preachers, I am not attacking anyone. He said it. I don't know who and I don't need to know.

Allow me to stress at this point, it is utterly and completely impossible for me to capture everything that took place during this period in the writings. Horrific events, chaos, pleasurable things are too numerous to mention. I'm sure there will be a dichotomy of opinions from the readers. Under the auspices of the Holy Spirit, the truth and nothing but the truth is being told. That has been stressed enough.

Pious is not a word that can be associated with me as a person, a Christian, a writer or in any way. Not holier than thou but merely human with many faults and making countless mistakes. Having the desire to serve God to the utmost as my number one goal in life propels me to complete this book and be a minister of the gospel—telling of God's goodness wherever I go. Now, having said that, let's continue.

On that same day, God said to me that He was not going to allow me to wear the pants in this relationship (That ended up being many). He told me that I would teach but I would take a back seat to my husband. Well, anyone who knows me know that taking a back seat to anyone just didn't quite sit well with me. Thus, one of many reasons a breaking was in order.

"When the Lord has built up Regina, then He shall appear in His glory" (Psalm 102:16). Actually, the scripture states, "When the Lord shall build up Zion, He shall appear in His glory". Has the building started? Far from it, the breaking is about to begin.

In March 1999, I resigned from the Social Security Administration in Minden, Louisiana; withdrew my retirement money and began an adventurous journey. My life began to change drastically from the life I was accustomed to. I became an outcast, invisible to many, ignored by most. Some told me that even the local preachers told them to stay away from me as I had lost my mind. Continue to read. You'll understand why they said what they said.

Aunt Clara Mae passed on April 3, 1999. Not fully understanding the root cause, I tend to avoid being around family members when a loved one has passed on. Knowing that absence from this body is to be present with the Lord, for those of us who are saved, has not lessened my avoidance still. During this time in my life I was deeply depressed and I suffered this time alone.

Later in the week, while visiting Bonnie who is a family member in Alexandria, La., I had the pleasure of going to the Christian

Worship Center. It was there I heard Rev. Kenneth Hagin speak. The message was so dynamic and the spirit was very much alive there. This was the first time in my life that I ever experienced laughing in the spirit. I couldn't stop and folks were laughing with me. My friend said that some were feeding off of me. I say they were feeding off of us. We were all high!

The Spirit was moving in ways I had never experienced before. There were people running, lifting their hands in praise, clapping and rejoicing in the Lord. At one point during the service I had laid my head on a man's shoulder sitting next to me and did not even realize it.

While visiting with Bonnie, I was cleaning and doing all kinds of things there when I had the audacity to ask God. "Lord, what am I, a servant?" His response was only one word—exactly. Okay, so I guess I know now. I'm going home.

While in Alexandria, my girlfriend said the Lord had spoken to her before I came and told her to give me some outfits. She said she asked him which ones and He responded "not all of them, just the ones with the price tags on them". She said she cried and cried as the outfits were too small for her but she definitely had plans of losing weight and getting back in them. Yet, she was obedient and I came away with a new wardrobe. Thanks Bonnie.

On a previous visit she just happened to have the exact Word Processor as I had been using at another friend's house that she was getting rid of. Who got it? Me.

The day of the funeral or home going service, while sitting at home, I asked God, "Where do I go from here? What do I read?" He said, Mark 11:23-24. After reading it, I heard "Speak to your mountain". What mountain? I knew there were so many? The response was all of them basically—lack, doubt and unbelief, fear, addiction to cigarettes, just to name a few. Saying something being super religious, I figured I had fulfilled my God given assignment. Double huh!!

It's April 14, 1999. I have visitors come who try to talk some sense in me regarding all that I was going through. The conversation shifted towards tithes. Questions were asked and lots of conversation followed regarding God's way of doing things in reference to tithes, seed sowing, and God's spoken word never contradicts His written word. I agree. I'm confused as to actually why we're even having this conversation. Hum??? "Beloved, believe not every spirit, but try the spirits whether they are of God; because many false prophets are gone out into the world." (I John 4:1)

As far as the tithe, I really couldn't understand the conversation as I had no income whatsoever at this point. I looked back over my tithes and offerings for the previous year and even though I missed a couple of times actually giving my quote, unquote tithe to the church, my actual giving financially far exceeded my tithes. I am a giver so you can understand my total confusion with this.

God shows me that not only will I be able to give my tithes and offerings but also sow into many other ministries. There is nothing more in life I enjoy than giving in one way or another. I live to give and I give to live. That's just me.

What's the significance of the scripture used above? Those that came said that the things I was saying and doing were not of God. They meant well however I knew that it wasn't me and I knew that I would constantly hear the voices, so it had to be God. Right? Remember God said that He was breaking me to build me up and He said that He was going to allow Satan to touch my life and that it would hurt. So, I admit, not everything that was said and done was God. Actually, it was allowed by Him because in a Christian's life Satan cannot touch us **Unless** God allows it.

I was told by others to ask my daughter her thoughts on all of this. In the natural it would have made perfect sense for me to stay on that job, work a few more years and retire. It was not like I was looking for a means of getting away from the job. I had a great job...one that I loved to do as it provided me another arena to help many less fortunate than myself. So, all I can say is I answered the call.

The next day I hear, "Could it be that what your Pastor was saying is true? Is it possible that you should return to your job?" Yes and yes.

Mentioning this to a friend of mine, I tell her how I am really confused. God has told me I'll write a book, do God's Storehouse and so many other things. I say to her, He's told me the book is, "To God Be the Glory." How does He get the glory? Her response was, "I believe He told you to do it but not yet". Did I move too soon?

During this time, while at the same person's house, I start to wonder, why I am always there cleaning and watching her prepare meals? Cooking has not been my thing. I'd rather clean any day than cook. That still small voice inside me said, "You should be watching and learning." I thought, no way, as I planned to cook as little as possible.

All throughout this period, I was at one house or another, cleaning and meddling. Cleaning has always been my forte. I got sick of cleaning, literally sick of and sick from cleaning. Meddling took me much longer but eventually I came to realize by meddling in other folks lives as I had been doing was hurting myself and hindering the works God was doing in their lives. It took me years to get to this revelation.

April 15, 1999 rolls around. God said to me on that day that I had been persecuted already and assured me that the persecutions were just beginning. He informed me that I would be persecuted many times for His sake. "Remember the word that I said unto you. The servant is not greater than his lord. If they have persecuted me, they will also persecute you..." (John 15:20)

Around this time God leads me to touch and agree with DI regarding the release of my money. He says to me then that Satan had his grips on my money as he knew I was going to sow seeds. We touched and agreed.

I am lead to go to Shreveport and deliver a package there. I have a teaspoon of gas in the car and no money, but I knew I could make it. When returning from Shreveport, I looked at the gas gauge and the light constantly came on. I was freaking out and I sung all the way home. I was singing "Doing the best I can with what I got. God can take a little and turn it into a lot..." I made it home. Thank you God! I sung, prayed, wiped sweat, and did a little of everything hoping to make it there.

Somewhere in all of this, I partnered with Trinity Broadcasting Network. I believed since I was being fed spiritually by them I should sow my seeds there. I also partnered with Creflo Dollar Ministries and many others during this time. Creflo became my spiritual father.

I sowed seeds targeted for fulfillment of the vision and dream; protection, healing and deliverance for my children and all of my family members; freedom from smoking; financial deliverance; restoration of broken relationships; generational blessings to begin and many other things.

Listening to a message concerning hearing from God, it was stated that whatever we hear from God is going to be wisdom. Also, Solomon's success was largely due to his being able to hear from God. That's a test for all Christians. God's sheep are supposed to hear His voice and not follow a stranger. The whole purpose to hearing God's voice is to follow Him. (Creflo Dollar Ministries, "Positioning Ourselves to Hear from God)

I spend a lot of time during this period, fasting and praying. A prayer list hangs throughout my houses no matter where I am pretty much at any given time. The list gets longer and longer.

This entire time God has also been preparing me to lose my Pops. He says at the time this wedding takes place, it will be a time of rejoicing and a time of mourning.

God leads me to be the caretaker for Pops assuring me that He will reward me for my efforts and obedience.

I hear messages about partnership. Unless there is a proven commitment, there is no covenant. Partnership is more than an association, it is a friendship.

Soaking in the bathtub, God says to me Satan has turned up the heat. He also told me that cigarettes would make me so sick I would regret the day I ever picked up a pack. Believe me, I did.

Reading everything in sight and believing I can do anything (well almost) I start to paint inside the house, outside the house and made a big mess painting a bathroom. DI persuaded me that I could paint the bathroom myself and not pay anyone to do it. It was awful. Even with having a drop cloth on the floor, Nikki and I had more paint on the floor than we did on the actual ceiling. That was all we were painting. DI came in and said to put the paint brushes down *now!* She said that she thought anyone could paint but Nikki and I proved her wrong. Oh well, don't tell me I can do something because I will try it.

April 23rd rolls around and after watching and listening to Bishop Eddie Long, God starts to ask me questions:

1) Could it be that Robert is not my best for you?
2) Is it possible the reason I didn't have you send Anthony's stuff back is because he's coming back?
3) Is it possible that your Pastor's helping to get him out is for you? (Him who?)
4) Is it possible that what Anthony, Dorothy and your Pastor say is true? (What?)

5) Is it possible I'll use Anthony in a mighty way in the ministry?
6) Is it possible that Anthony was not my

husband then and is now?
7) Could it be I am doing a breaking in your church to build it up?
8) I've shown you visions and dreams of your church growing in leaps and bounds. Could it be I'll use the both of you to accomplish this? (Who?)

He asked me a few others. Then He said to me, "Regina, I can do anything I want to bless you and I can use anyone I want and do it any way I want to." Okay.

The last question He asked me was, "Could it be that DI and I didn't know as much as we thought we did?" You know the answer to all.

Moving right along now, April 24th, I do a house dedication and invite some others as we prayed over my house and dedicated it to the works of the Lord. After the prayer of dedication, each person pronounced a blessing over the property. There were only five of us there. That five was enough. This was the beginning of "God's Storehouse" which you will read more about in Chapter Six.

To provide a bit of insight, "God's Storehouse" or the vision God gave is one of providing technical assistance on various matters relating to business; information and referral services, temporary housing to those who find themselves displaced due to reasons beyond their control and emergency services in the form of furniture, dishes, pots, pans, etc., to newlyweds or those rebuilding their lives after loss. The mission of "God's Storehouse" was later established as "To holistically meet the social and spiritual needs of those in our community or connect them with resources that can." More will follow. It was and is about each community taking care of its own through collaborations and partnerships. You will get a more in-depth view in chapter 6. Back to now.

Janet and Leroy were the first to get married on May 8, 1999. Her colors were red, black, gold and white. She marched in on the song, "The Lady, Her Lover and Her Lord". Our family came together and she had a really nice ceremony.

Our cousin Dee Dee made her dress. That girl can make anything and I do mean anything. She is so gifted and talented in so many areas. She can look at something, draw a pattern, make it and it looks like it came out of the store.

May 23, 1999

I get a letter in the mail from Anthony telling me he is being released from jail and asking about reconciliation. After reading the letter, God spoke to me and said, "Anthony is being released as He was about to call His mother home." He has told me several times over that Anthony's mother will not be here to hear him do his first sermon.

He reminded me again today of the fact that He is calling my Pops home soon. He assured me that He is the only Father I will ever need. He said to me then that He is building up His army of people and that there are thousands in Louisiana who will support me. He told me to be ready at the drop of a hat to do presentations about God's Storehouse. He has told me by the time things are actually up and running He will have called my Pops home.

God said to me that He is going to richly bless all of those who are obedient to Him, both spiritually and financially. He said businesses will spring forth from "God's Storehouse", successful businesses He said. He also said that it is time for all of the promises to take place—the wedding (not necessarily mine either), the completion of the book, the new businesses emerging, my first message being delivered and Glory.

June 1, 1999

God tells me He has now broken me as far as the handling of my finances, my cocky attitude towards men, and in every way. He said He would now send me all the money and everything else I need and that I am not to borrow anything else from anyone. Relieved says it mildly. I have never, ever liked borrowing money from others. I like to be the giver.

All throughout this ordeal I have borrowed money from different ones. He now says it's time to pay it all back. He says that you have money that you are not even aware of and it is coming.

He said to me in reference to the husband He has for me, I will now be as humble as a lamb as I now know no real man will bow down to me. He told me that I already love him and he already loves me. He told me it's the end...the end of being broke, the end of chasing men, the end of trying to have things my way, the end of a lot of things.

With so much happening and so little understanding, there were many times I wanted to throw in the towel. Pleading and begging with God became something that took place many times throughout this period...begging to be released from all of this. Saying to Him one day I am tired and I just cannot do this anymore, He responded, "There are too many lives at stake here". He assured me that this is not about me, or me and a husband, it's about Him and kingdom building.

That same day He told me that I now have to trust Him for everything, to bring money to me, to bring the people to me and to bring me everything I need. I know I do.

All this time I thought I was the bomb, all that and a bag of chips. It can be a very humbling experience to realize that one isn't all that. If anyone knows how to break a person it's God. When people tell you some things about yourself you can kind of shrug it off. But when God tells you, what can you do but humble yourself. "If my people which are called by my name would humble themselves and pray and seek My face and turn from their wicked ways, then will I hear from heaven and heal the land."

June 2, 1999

I started seeing my daughter and me moving back to California. I did not want to go to California. I wanted to stay in Louisiana.

Okay, so God has also spoken to me that at the same time that He has been breaking me, He has been breaking His best for me as well. My brother told me a long time ago that I could not share my visions and dreams with everyone. Did that stop me? You know it didn't. I wanted people to believe first without seeing. Isn't that faith?

June 4, 1999

God shares with me that DI (who became many) is going to go through a breaking also as she has to learn to submit to her husband. He assures me that there are two things still He has to break me from. Guess what they are—cigarettes and diet cokes. All I can say is break me.

God tells me you are going to learn to just say no. Not knowing what He meant you know I asked. Well, He said just say no to handouts and yes to blessings. What's a handout? Anytime a person does something for one and that person has begged for the crumbs from the table, so to speak, that is a handout. Anytime a person does something for one grudgingly or of necessity, that is a handout because God loves a cheerful giver.

Some may or may not believe this, but each and every time something in the way of utilities was cut off, He prepared me in advance and had a place for me to stay. Lights, gas, cable, telephone…all were cut off at various times throughout this process.

You want to know what's really awesome about all of this. Even though these were cut off numerous times over a four year period, each time a person or family came to me for food, I was able to give it to them. Every time a person or family came to me for technical assistance, I made myself available to provide it. Each time a person came for furniture, dishes and the like, I was able to provide it. Each time a person came for a word and prayer, I was able to and gladly provided it. Yet, I couldn't help myself.

There would be praise parties going forth from that place with no utilities on. I would have meetings and have "To God Be the Glory" celebrations with not a light on. Now you why know people thought I had lost my mind.

People would look at me and pity me. I became so faith filled that I always responded to anyone who asked, it's easy to have faith when times are going well but the real test of one's faith is when they aren't, so I'd praise Him.

My family members must have been as strange as I because most times I'd ask them to come and they'd be there. We would praise God together. For a while, we met together, prayed together, ate together, learned together. Division and separation came, but we did get on track.

God speaks to my heart that I am an asset, not a liability. He says that I'm writing a book that will be published and read throughout the world. He tells me I'm about to appear in an International magazine, thanks to Him and once the book is published

I will speak to millions of people as He has made sure I will go on Trinity Broadcasting Network.

I keep trying to shorten this but for some reason I cannot. The story has to be told. Hopefully you're still with me.

Saturday, June 5, 1999 2:43 AM

God speaks. Who is mere man than any of you can figure me out? My ways are not your ways. My thoughts are not your thoughts. My time is not your time. He said to me to stop telling people certain things He was telling me and showing me. He said people are starting to think I'm strange again and at this point this is not what He wants.

He said to me that He uses other people to meet one's needs and that I didn't have to try to understand it but just be obedient. He said, "Your Pastor told you to rise above what others say or think and be obedient to me. He was right. Continue to do so.

God assured me that He loves me and only wants to start the building process now. He said for me to not turn down any blessings that comes my way—not handouts, blessings.

He said that He is breaking all over, not just with me but a lot of people as He is building them up as well. Christians, according to God, are being broken worldwide to get to the point where he or she surrenders to Him and Him only. He said, "It's your time now, but after awhile some of the same people who think you are strange will start to experience some of the same things that you are going through". He assured me some will think them strange.

God said to me that He has given me the gift of prophesy which is for the edification and building up of people, but I am also a prophetess and this is why He shows me the good as well as the bad. He says He shows me the bad to warn people and to intercede in prayer for them. He said they don't understand now but they will later.

God said to me, "Your Pastor is a mighty man of God. He's modest but I'm going to bless him in spite of him. He doesn't want recognition, but I am going to recognize him because he has a good heart and truly wants to serve me and spread the gospel. There are so many others within your church that I am about to bless. They are going through a breaking process as well. Rest assured, they won't think you strange then". (During this breaking period I actually had three Pastors and all were and are mighty men of God)

During this time, God told me that some family members would send me money. I asked for fifteen hundred dollars. He said that I would not need it and for me to give it to two other family members as they need it as they put themselves out on a limb to help me and they are now in need of finances. I said to Him, "Whenever it comes in, I'll do it".

They actually went out on a limb many times to help me and I did the same for them. I believe the incident specifically referred to came in November 2006. Read on. He said to me, "Kendrick has not been in this book much but he will be soon".

God thanked me for being obedient as He said if I did not obey Him, I could die a spiritual and a physical death. He told me that I would never have to worry about money again. He said all of the remaining work that now needed to be done will be done by professionals.

Why did He thank me for being obedient? I got back to work on learning more things to help myself and others. I quit a few times.

I saw my bills go down to almost nothing and then skyrocket in pursuit of this vision; overdrawn on my bank account so often. I thought people would come in and support this endeavor I thought because this was a vision from God and it was about helping people that others would readily jump on board. I thought, I thought, I thought, and was wrong so much.

Pledges were made based on promises from others to do things. Promises to provide services in one fashion or another were made based on promises made from others. It *is* better to put your trust in God than to put confidence in man. Each and every time I made a promise based on what man said (at first), I was let down. Lessons were learned.

September 10, 1999

Today I made a covenant with God. I promised Him that I would not speak things just for the sake of pleasing people when I know that He has told me something. I made an agreement that I would stand no matter what. I made a vow that I would trust Him and not man. The promise that I made to God was from that day forward I would seek His face, listen for His voice, read His word and be obedient, no matter what. His promise to me was that He would supply every need I have, watch over and protect me and give me all the promises that His word says I can have. I can handle that.

Later in the day, He speaks…"If Robert wants to borrow money from UC Lending or anyone else, let him do it. You won't need money then. If Robert wants the trucking company, let him come to you for help. If Robert wants or needs money from your Pops, let him come to you and ask (He assured me he would not need anything from him). Let Robert handle the business. Don't be in the middle trying to arrange the outcomes of anything. Let Robert handle the business." I hear you loud and clear.

Later in September, I heard that it's time for me to return to work for the Social Security Administration. Okay. He assured me then that I was going back to work for the Social Security Administration. I thought it would be Minden but I ended up in beautiful Torrance, California. When did this happen? About four years later.

He did tell me that there was still much for me to learn and that He was sending me away from Minden to learn more and after this I would go back and teach His people. He said I would tell of His goodness and I will.

On September 23rd, I had a dream. In this dream, I was looking over a huge city like Los Angeles. The Lord spoke in the dream and said as far as your eyes can see and then some is yours. Not knowing what any of this meant, I just said okay.

Here is an important lesson I'll share. Earlier, I touched on it now I'll go into a bit more. People, be **Careful** with who you call a friend. A real, true friend is someone who knows you, knows all about you, your faults as well as your strengths and still loves you in spite of. A real friend is one that stays when the rest of the world walks away. That's a friend.

Here's another tip for those aspiring to be writers. Keep a journal! Write it down. I thought early on that I was just writing my thoughts and my day-to-day actions. It was only later that I realized the writings were the makings of the book.

Keep a list of the things you are thankful to God for and when the enemy comes in, read the list and start to praise God. Are you in good health? Write it there. Got a job? Write it down. Are your children and family members doing well? Write it down. The list will become so long that once you even start to think about complaining or entertaining any negative thoughts, a review of the blessings will have you praising God like crazy. That's a high better than any drug or alcoholic beverage.

Dance for the Lord. Shake the devil off and just dance. Shackles will be broken.

Now we move into October. The actual date is October 22, 1999. Now, it is at this point that God tells me that my friend is ashamed as he has done a lot of negative talk. He tells me that he doesn't realize that he needs me yet but he will soon.

God says to me that there were a few people who have wronged me and in order for them to return to right standing with Him, they will have to right the wrongs. He let's me know that "God's Storehouse" is a lifetime ministry for me.

He shares that Nikki's last name is going to change and her dad won't mind at all. He tells me that Kendrick is going to live with Chris for a while (His biological mother).

As we proceeded a bit further, it's now October 23, 1999 and I hear, "The only way Satan deceived you during this breaking period is in your believing I created a need. I didn't but I have allowed Satan to though. You will no longer use others as crutches. Everything that has happened has been a part of the plan. You have been in training for ministry."

October 27, 1999

On this day God tells me, or rather reminds me that the family members He mentioned before are sending me the money and for me to always remember that even though I have many family members to never, put anyone's needs before those in my household first. He said to put Him first, then take care of my immediate family's needs and then extend it to others. God had to show me that even having money set aside for miscellaneous expenses is His will. Don't talk about me, pray for me. I always thought if I had anything left over I should give it away. That can be true and cannot be. It's true only if He says or leads me to give it away. Otherwise it's false.

November 7, 1999

I guess I just feel like writing now. I miss being in church so bad it hurts. How can I go through when they mock and make fun of me because I continually say, "God said"? I've got to go. My life depends on it.

The thing that I don't believe anyone realizes is that, yes; I'll be the first to admit that I am strange. I'm also human. I have the same desires and temptations as anyone else. Loving the Lord has just become my main love relationship. I still seek to be loved, accepted and understood by others. Clowning around is something I love to do. Entertaining is another thing. Nobody comes around much.

November 13, 1999

God tells me that there will be many people who make investments that won't make a dime. He said they won't lose anything because they won't put up anything. He did say that those who have invested in me or sown seeds into my life will now reap the benefits. He also said that those who don't make money from the investments, I will bless.

He said to me, "I would not allow you to buy a microwave, vacuum cleaner, living room set or any of the other things that Robert has already as Robert's furniture will come into your house. (I got all these things and more from a person named Robert in California years later).

I am not going to build you and your husband up apart, but together." He says that I need to look ahead and quit looking back; to remember Lot's wife. He tells me that he has heard my prayers for Kendrick and that He has already answered them. Going on, He says that Kendrick is my son as He gave him to me.

I start to hear that Anthony is Robert and then Anthony is not Robert. Who's talking?

Now, the Holy Spirit ministers to my heart and tells me to remember to invite him in daily as he is a gentleman and will not walk in or force his way in uninvited.

I hear, "Regina, you will continue to give until the day you leave this earth, but you now know my order for giving. You are loved much by God. You are loved much by many. God has shown His love for you. It is time for others to show their love. Pray without ceasing. Pray in tongues. Have regular praise parties. Study, and study some more. Tell of God's goodness. Shout it from the rooftops."

"Regina, get ready, your husband, my best for you is coming and this time he wants to marry you. You don't have to call him at all. God and I already made that phone call. Congratulations. Today is your day for a miracle. Now you will see my power."

All during the entire waiting/breaking period, I watched Creflo & Taffi Dollar, Joyce Meyer, Juanita Bynum, Bishop T. D. Jakes, and Dr's. I. V. & Bridgett Hilliard, Paula White and many others on Trinity Broadcasting Network. Being fed the word daily by such powerful and dynamic preachers and teachers helped me to grow tremendously. Creflo Dollar actually became my spiritual father. I lived to hear the messages of hope and encouragement received from these dynamic leaders.

Joyce Meyer's life story and mine actually bear many similarities. Certain parts of Juanita Bynum's life, I could relate to. Paula White came on the scene and I thought, "My God, these women were messed up and I can relate to all of them. Is there that much really wrong with me?" A resounding yes!

But the ultimate message of wholeness after brokenness offered hope to a hurting woman. It was during this time that I began to believe in God; to believe in myself and the possibilities of my pursuing many long buried dreams (or so I thought they were). I began to speak a new way. Speaking as if I were a King's kid and anything and everything was mine for the asking. That angered and upset a few folks. Especially when most of the time that I was talking,

I most likely didn't have two nickels to rub together. That's okay. I had vision!

Delusions of grandeur? Yes, I was accused of having them. You might ask "Why?" I'm so glad you asked. The reason for the accusation is that I dared to dream of pulling myself out of the rut I was in; to dream of helping others achieve their goals, visions and dreams in life; to dream of being blessed to be a blessing to others. I dared to dream and like Joseph I told my dreams and visions to others. Needless to say, it was too late to take the sting away after telling it and telling it. Ostracized by my own people, I sought solitude in the word and through the Trinity Broadcasting Network.

God continually reminds me about my need to quit smoking. He reminds me constantly of my need to get my finances in order His way, according to the word. He reminds me that He made them male and female. He reminds me that ***the husband*** is the head of the wife as Christ is the head of the church. He reminds me that it is not Burger King and I can't have it my way. He reminds me that unless HE builds the house, they labor in vain that built it. He reminds me of my need to feed the hungry—spiritual and physical food; to visit those in prison; to clothe the naked.

He reminds me constantly that two are better than one. He reminds me that sexual promiscuity is definitely not His way. His way—flee fornication. Marriage is honorable unto all and the bed undefiled. He reminds me of so much. How does He remind me? Through both His written and spoken word.

Now don't think that God hasn't been reminding you as well. He reminds all of us through the reading of our roadmap—the **<u>B I B L E.</u>**

God had a long battle ahead. It took me more than seven years of going through many trials and making many mistakes to finally come to the point where I was ready to say, "Okay Lord, nevertheless, not my will but yours be done". Seven years of going through. Seven years of wondering and wandering. Seven years of being broken, molded, shaped and reshaped. Seven years of falling down and getting back up. Seven long years! Those seven years have seemed liked an eternity.

People, I wrestled with God so much that at times I would wish He'd just give up on me. After all, the price was too much to pay. It costs a lot to deny self and follow Jesus. It costs a lot when one doesn't fully understand all that is happening in their lives yet try to explain it to others. It costs a lot but the cost is nothing compared to the rewards received later.

One way I could have avoided some negative things taking place was by just keeping my big mouth shut. I talk too much most of the time. That's a whole *"nuther"* chapter or book. Pardon the slang.

Progressing to the dated materials, In May of 1999, after I had spoken to several people telling them that God said I was getting married, a relative told me of an article she had recently read. In the article, God had promised the woman a husband and had told her that she would marry this particular man and when the marriage would occur. The woman did not even know anyone by that name but several years later, the wedding took place just as He said it would and she married the man He said she would. What message should I get from this? If you thought, "If God said it, them it must be right." Whatever the "it" may be. You are so wrong. There were so many times that I began to question whether or not I actually heard from God what I thought or rather knew I had heard. I was somewhat accustomed to the Burger King mentality so when things didn't go as I thought or happen when I thought, the fight was on!!!

I am trying so hard to get away from 1999 but there is still more that needs to be told. It is definitely not my intent to bore you with my rambling on...

Let's see if I can capture the really hot points in the next two pages and move at least into 2000. When God said tell the story, it seems He means for it to be told. There is so much to tell.

God tells me that this man loves me. He tells me that I'll meet his family and he'll meet mine. He tells me that his sister will love me. He tells me that this man really likes my legs. He tells me *again* how I need to quit smoking as no man is going to want to kiss an ashtray. He tells me He is breaking me in reference to finances, my dealings with men, the smoking of the cigarettes and the diet cokes. Don't ask.

He tells me when the husband He has for me come in I will be as humble as a lamb as I now know no real man will bow down to me. At this point, I must say I never expected anyone to actually bow down to me. I had just suffered from some really bad relationships and had vowed to God and myself to not let another man hurt me as I had been hurt in the past.

When I wanted to throw in the towel and just give up, God constantly reminded me that it is not about me and that there are too many lives at stake. He said it is so much bigger than a husband and I.

Now all the time He is telling me about my marriage and wedding taking place, it seems that everyone around me is getting married but me. What about me? My cousin marries. Guess where the wedding takes place? My house. Oops—"God's Storehouse".

My son marries. Guess where the wedding takes place? My god daughter marries, you know the question. All of these weddings take place there and who does the decorating, planning, coordinating and so on. Me, along with the prospective brides, that's who. And, with them taking place there at the house, the cleanup afterwards was pretty much my responsibility. I like to clean. Right? Huh!!! I'm tired and I'm wondering when will my turn come? Well, now I really don't care.

I've gotten so sick of hearing about a husband I could just puke. Not being sacrilegious I was just plain tired. This all started months ago and boy was I ready for it to end. Who needs a man? The Bible states a man who finds a wife findeth a good thing. (Proverbs 18:22) Where does it say a woman who finds a husband finds a good thing? Being a godly wife is real work! From a Biblical standpoint, looking at Proverbs 31, that virtuous woman worked hard. "Her husband is known in the gates, when he sitteth among the elders of the land (Proverbs 18:23). Okay, she's doing all of this hard work and he is known in the gates. You understand the need for breaking in reference to men now, right?

A "Godly Woman" has to train and teach younger women, both those chronologically and spiritually younger. There are a couple of scriptures that come to mind to support this. They are found in Titus 2:3-5 and the one that states to whom much is given much is required found in Luke 12:48.

September 9, 1999

Today I have watched Joyce Meyer and Bishop Frank Reid on the Trinity Broadcasting Network and I am on a high. I have several affirmations, poems, and quotes in my office that I read daily. As I sit here and meditate on the word of God seeking direction for my life, there is such an aura of peace. It's only when I get in the flesh that the peace leaves. (Thou wilt keep thee in perfect peace whose mind is stayed on thee). I encourage you to surround yourself with the word of God and other materials of encouragement to help you along life's way. Dwell not in the valley of despair. Believe it; God *does* know what's best for us.

Thank God for the good as well as the bad. You will find that in every situation, as a Christian, what the devil means for bad, God means it for our good. Know who and whose you are. Take the limits off of God. The word of God says, with God *nothing* is impossible. Believe it and receive it. God does it all for His glory.

Don't try to justify yourself to people. People really have no heaven or hell to put you in. Be someone who pleases God and not a people *"pleaser"*.

Work daily to improve yourself; to improve your relationship with God. Put Him first and then go about doing enjoying life. There has to be balance in life.

Mentor someone, young or old. Become really involved in people's lives (not meddling). Add value to people. There are no big *"I's"* and little *"You's"*; we are all God's children and each are called to use what He's given for kingdom building.

The following poem was actually written a few years later but I believe this is the place it should be—

Alone

Never in my life have I felt so all alone
As I have the past few years
Never have I been so misunderstood
Nor shed so many tears

I've often believed, truly all of my life
One should love unconditionally
Well, today my Father in heaven above
Has finally set me free

You see, love to me has never been
About possessions or material things

It's always been first and foremost
Introducing folks to the King

Life is so precious and time is so near
That people have got to know
That God and family are what matters most
And tell it wherever they go
Life, too many, may be a game
There's nothing further from the truth
God _is_ in control of people,
places, things & time
Just ask Samuel, Esther or Ruth

Folks, get real, time is winding up
Swallow your pride
Put it aside
Let's all drink of the Master's cup

We each must learn to be good stewards
Over that we now have
By sharing with others the things
that we know
People will no longer thirst
Always remember, number one,
no matter what
Is ALWAYS put God first

Put God first in your time,
your talents, your all
It's His rightful place
Shower His love on all you meet
So all may one day see His face

Never forget where you have been
And never look down on others
That addict, wino, prostitute, whatever
May possibly be your sister or brother

Don't be so heavenly minded
That you're no earthly good
Be yourself, Be real
And it will be as it should

Even if you're misunderstood by folks
Don't worry and never fret
Because God is saying to you and them
It ain't quite over yet

Don't look at what you think you see
Looks can be so deceiving
Uplift, encourage all you meet and
Tell them to keep believing

It saddens my heart so much to know
That many who read God's word
Don't believe the word they read
Nor the word that they have heard

God has a plan for each of our lives
And He never changes that
It's our willingness & obedience
And our willingness to forget

In me, I have no spirit of fear

Nor spirit of any shame
I have boldly and loudly proclaimed
All rise in Jesus name

The shame should come on the part
Of those who rejected His word
But even in spite of what's been said & done
His messengers will be heard
Now I am not saying to any of you
That God wants us to work alone
I am saying I'll continue to do my part
By mail, by mouth and by phone

Each of us longs to hear
When we meet the Master face to face
Well done thy good and faithful one
You have finally finished the race.

    Want the best that God has to give you. You will know that you've really matured as a child of God when you want the best for everyone you meet as well. Never, ever think you know it all. When we leave this life here there will still be much that we don't know.

    Develop a lifetime of learning, a thirst for knowledge. God's people are destroyed for lack of knowledge. Have you ever heard the saying what you don't know can't hurt you? That's the biggest lie! What you don't know can not only hurt you but kill you. Learn, stretch, and grow!

    At this point I want to encourage you to **Dare to Dream**; to **Soar with the Eagles**. Surround yourself with people who add to your life. Watch what you say. Death and life is in the power of the tongue. There is so much power in our words. And, once you've been fed, feed someone else encouraging, uplifting words. What can a brother or sister do for me? They can help me to be the best person that I can be and I, in turn, can help someone else.

If one person wants to venture out and start a business, buy a house, or etc. I encourage you to do it. All new adventures start with a dream or a vision. Most large corporation started as a thought in someone's mind and started small. Don't despise the days of small beginnings. Dreams do have a way of becoming reality. It all boils down to choices, mainly "how bad do you want it?" Once the decision is made then put some legs to your faith. God is no respecter of person and if He ever did it for one, He can and will do it for you. Take the limits off of Him.

Okay, I've preached enough. Let's get back to the dated entries. Let's fast forward to December 1999. You'll find that even though I inserted the poem above, I really did not get to the full understanding of parts of it until so much later.

I cannot skip over November 26, 1999. It was on that day that God asked me a question and I did not know the answer to it. The question was, "Why do you want to help people who have hurt you?" He also spoke and said I am too trusting of people. Well, the answer to the first one was (being biblically correct or so I thought)…the Bible says we are blessed to be a blessing in Genesis. And, it also states bless those who curse you and pray for those who despitefully use you. To the latter I said, "God it's not the people I trust so much. I only trust you". (He knew I was trusting people entirely too much) *It is better* to put your trust in God than to put confidence in man.

Often times I was thought of as a person who overly gave, in turn invited many opinions. What puzzled me was, the same people who would constantly remind me that I was too generous would readily accept whatever I offered them. It was only when my giving was connected with others that I became too giving. Go figure.

Some told me repeatedly how I allowed others to take advantage of me. I did. But, as you will read later it was all a part of the process. God directed me with practically every dime I gave away. Oh yes, Satan did deceive me in some cases as far as my giving but not too many.

We are all instruments to be used by God. I now know that I have to be prayerful as to whom to assist, when to do it and all that. Being a giver by nature the enemy will take the same thing that God has gifted you with and try to deceive one. Satan knows our weaknesses so it's best to stay prayed up. Pray without ceasing.

God has used and continues to use me to bless many others and many to bless me and for that I say "thank you". Every day is a day of Thanksgiving. We should not wait for the one day a year set aside to celebrate the blessings or to give thanks but should do it daily.

Life, children, families and friends are all blessings from God.

You know people made fun of me, made negative comments and sometimes even to my face and said all kinds of things that really hurt. There was no way I could explain to people what was happening but I tried to often. I felt I had to defend myself. It was only later that I realized that this battle was not even mine to fight.

I never want to interfere in someone's life when I know God is dealing with it so when God says no, I say no…well, not yet but I finally get there later. I also want to stress this. If God tells me to give away a house (which He did), to give away a car (which He did), to give away all my worldly possessions (which He had me give most of them away) I would do it in a heartbeat. Because when He says it

I know that these are seeds sown for greater things to take place. When? Later. He provides seed to the sower.

WARNING—Know that it's God, and then go for it. As long as the earth remains, there will forever be seed, time and harvest. Not exactly as the Bible shows it but I specifically separated seedtime into two words as once a seed is sown it takes time for the harvest to come, but it will.

Now to those who think you can come to me and say God said give you this or that, my only response to you is I'll pray and let Him direct me. His sheep do know His voice and another one they will not follow. So, don't think you'll be able to pull that one on me.

Honestly, no one has used me. I've just been taught some valuable lessons (not yet). God gives each of us as Christians, money with a mission. He wants us all to be distribution centers. He gives us talents and gifts with a mission. Everything we have belongs to Him. The word says every good and perfect gift comes from God. We are merely stewards.

A steward oversees or manages what belongs to someone else. The Bible states the earth is the Lord's and the fullness thereof, the world and they that dwell therein. We have nothing. We are just temporarily loaned people and things from Him.

We must be willing to say to God, "Whatever you tell me to do is exactly what I'm going to do." and mean it. I'm here to tell you dying to flesh and getting to that point takes a while, that is if you're stubborn and hardheaded and have a Burger King mentality. Understanding will come later. Later can be days, months or even years, but it will come.

How many of you have had God come down from heaven and hand you the money, food, clothing, shelter, whatever you need

Himself? Who does He use? When you ask a friend or acquaintance to let you have something you just know you need and they tell you no, how many of you have seen God extend deadlines or have someone come to you with the exact thing you've been needing or wanting? I have too many times to mention.

Have you ever gotten real holy and just prayed to God for hours telling Him what you think you need and how you need it and He shows you that you don't need it at all? Sometimes I think God just listens to us pour out our hearts to Him telling Him all that we just have to have and then in His infinite wisdom shows us we don't need it anyway. But, back to the earlier questions…God uses people to bless people. Read your Bible. It is in the word.

Check this out. Have you ever been sitting minding your own business and "something" (as people love to say) told you to call someone or go and buy a card or purchase something for someone and take it to them or even give away money when you may only have little? Who is that something? I choose to believe that something is God. Thus, my saying God said for me to do this or God led me to do this.

Okay, so I'm in the flow now. What about the times you've seen an outfit or a pair of shoes and you really want them but don't have the money and **Suddenly** out of the blue someone walks up to you and hands you the exact thing you need or wanted. ***Awesome God!!***

Running

I have run so in circles
I've run myself ragged
Trying to do much for others
While neglecting my own

I have cared much for others
And when I've needed help
All I ever got

Was mostly left alone

Being left alone was not bad
It made me realize many things
I've been hurt, wounded and sad
But I drew closer to the King

My heart's desires is to save the world
Truthfully, I can't save myself
That doesn't stop me from wanting to share
With all that I meet
As all may enter into wealth

Wealth to some, may be possessions
It may be material things
But you know that wealth to me is family
And a right relationship with the King

My children have suffered
We've been the laugh of the town
We've been denied and deprived of so much

But what we got in return is priceless
As we each received the Master's touch

God has a way of turning things around
In His own way and time
I believe it is time we leave this town

And let Him handle this place
He can do it so much better than I
And with Him, there will be no disgrace

So folks my message today is to you
I've tried and I've tried and I've tried
And now I am not willing to try anymore
As in trying, I cried and I cried
God is love and God is truth
And by trying to get help from you
I found myself along the way
And now I have much work to do

Work in getting my life together in every area and all aspects
When that happens I believe then and only then
Will I get real respect?

When I love, I really do love hard
And for me what's surprising the most is
I always believed LOVE would return
Not nightmares or ghosts

So, as of today I say farewell
And a big hello to the future
No longer will I allow others to pull my bell
I'll simply start a new venture

It is November 29th at 6:14 am. I am up and typing. Following my usual routine, (when I had lights and cable) I watched Creflo Dollar and did some reading. God speaks to me, "Regina, I know you are tired. You have been obedient all the way. I am tired of people holding up My (God) program and I will bless you with whomever you choose. Everyone can be replaced. This depends on people's willingness **and** obedience." God doesn't force His will on anyone. If He did all would be saved.

On December 3, 1999, Anthony (my second and third husband) and I made the decision for the umpteenth time that we would focus on being friends. One thing he said to me was that I was the person who taught him what unconditional love means. He said when he messed up and I showed him kindness it really messed with his head.

Anthony, when bound by the drug addiction, would take everything that wasn't nailed down, pawn it or sell it and then tell me where to go to get it. I bought back my things so many times over no wonder I stayed in the hole. This was during the course of the marriages.

Once he had taken the car and pulled his usual—gone for days. I had to walk places so much and was making car payments *myself*. You know that didn't sit too well with me. This particular time when he came home, I could not for the life of me yell, scream obscenities at him (Yes, you heard me right. This was prior to the breakings), or any of that. I asked him if he was hungry and was actually going to fix him food minus the rat poison. He said no real quick. I promise I had no intentions of harming him.

Seriously though, we realized that we are just too much alike. He will give a person the shirt off his back. He is a giver.

With him, like me, no one is a stranger. I'll forever love this man. I may not like some of his ways and I know he doesn't like some of mine but I will forever love him.

I believe it is the differences in people that make the wholeness. I also believe in a marriage relationship or a partnership, where one is weak the other should be strong. Two people, in my humble opinion, that have the same weaknesses can help each other much. A marriage between two with the exact same weaknesses, well, I don't know.

I guess I've mentioned Robert or a few of them. Well when I first met the "Robert", it was Rev. Robert White. During this period, even though most times we could not stand each other, I actually started to care for him, and as with Anthony, I'm sure it's until death do us part thing as well.

It would be negligent on my part to not state that the reason I was able to do a lot of the things for others in Louisiana that I did was largely due to his support during this time. Without his help and the help of my natural family members, I could not have done any of this. So, again, I say thanks to all of you. You know who you are.

Love— a four letter word that many people don't have a clue as to what it means. Many of us know that the definition of love is found in I Corinthians 13. But what is love really? Love is action. Love is not something that is talked, it is something shown. It is accepting a person for who they are; seeing the good in that person even when they don't see it and believing in that person.

Love is defending someone when others try to put them down. It is not engaging in backbiting, ditch digging or anything that defames the character of another.

> ***The Bible says, "God is love. Perfect love cast out fear. How can we say we love God whom we've never seen and hate our brother? Thou shalt love the love thy God with all thy heart...thou shalt love thy neighbor as thyself."***

There is so much in the Word about love. Read the Word. There's some good stuff in it.

Let's elaborate a little on the second greatest commandment...thou shalt love thy neighbor as thyself. What I get out of this is first you have to love yourself before you can show unconditional love to someone else. Loving you means having self-respect. It means being able to say "no" when you need to without feeling guilty. It means looking in the mirror saying to yourself, no matter what shape, color or size you are, "I love myself". It means approving of yourself and not allowing others to define you. It means recognizing and appreciating your own uniqueness. Loving yourself means understanding that you are and will continue to be, a work in progress. Then when you get to that point you can give out unconditional love to others.

Loving yourself also means knowing when to back away from deadly or disastrous relationships. Everyone is not going to be on your front row. So, please don't confuse what I'm saying into a means of bondage. Loving yourself is being free to live as you believe and allowing others the same privilege.

I could write a whole book on love but I'll close this part with this, loving you means having boundaries and balance.

Are you tired of reading now? Put the book down a minute or an hour or however long, relax and come back when you're refreshed.

Let's get back to some more dated entries.

December 6, 1999

God speaks to me, "Regina, you went through your break down to get your life in order. Today is a very important day in your life. It is time for some changes. Don't be surprised if some of the people you thought were going to do some things change to others. Don't be surprised. On Friday, I told you to get ready for some change. Now your life is changing in a really big way." Another thing He said to me was to rest as my life was about to turn into a whirlwind of activities.

God said He wanted Nikki and me to rest as things are going to happen suddenly and we will both beg for rest. He said, "I want you to trust Me. Get a paper daily. Send flowers, sympathy cards, congratulations cards and others as I lead you to. I am putting you in touch with ALL of the people who will help further MY cause."

December 21, 1999

"Regina, you have gone to your own and your own received you not. You will not beg or plead with anyone to help them. If the people of Minden want your help, let them ask you. You are not ready yet to go forward. Keep listening to me and do as I instruct you to do. Don't try to force your way on anyone. I know you've heard the message "The Violent Take it by Force" but I have already made the way. The people of Minden will want and need your help. Just be patient. Well done thy good and faithful servant. You have been faithful over few things, I am now making you ruler over much. Anthony is not your husband. Yes, I am going to use Anthony mightily in ministry and yes, Anthony will soon be free from drugs forever and yes, you will help Anthony much and he you. But, no, Regina you will not marry Anthony".

You know one definition of blessed is empowered to prosper. Every time I would sing the song, "I Am Blessed", I was actually singing that into existence. Death and life is in the power of the tongue. Thank you, Rev. Victor Carter for giving me that song.

People, in my book, all of the men I've listed thus far are my heroes. Each and every one of them came into my life at different times and helped me tremendously. There were others like Willie James Bradford, Willie Gene Richardson, Willie T. Richardson—men in the family that helped with picking up and delivering furniture and in just numerous ways... unsung heroes.

One lady had this saying, drop that zero and get you a hero. I honestly don't know any zeroes at all. That's the truth.

Finally, we've made it to the year 2000!!! My birthday comes and goes. A couple of friends take me out and did we have a great time? Yes, thanks Ed and Charlotte.

Anthony has left for California and is still searching. I can totally empathize with him. He is walking in fear of the unknown.

Now, let's talk a bit about relationships. Some men out there have really good wives and just don't appreciate them. (Yes, this is included in the daily writings—January 10, 2000 to be exact) They, the men, never take their wives out to dinners or movies or anything. They fail to romance their wives and take them for granted. Some don't include wives in important decisions.

Men purchase their expensive toys and spend more time with them than the wives God gave them. Birthdays, anniversaries, Valentine's Day—these are all special to women. Treat us with "just because" days—just because you think about us and care, we love them. Surprise us with flowers, cards or an unplanned evening on the town.

We as **virtuous** women will in return work with you to help you to be the best man ever. We will encourage, support you in all areas, clean and cook for you, keep you looking and smelling good, do sensible shopping, massage your backs when you're tired. Am I right, virtuous women?

Don't take us for granted just because we say "I do". Don't say, "I stop" when we say those two magical words. It's a partnership. A three fold cord is not easily broken.

Men, allow Christ to be the head of your lives. Read the word. Listen with your hearts for His voice and instructions. You're to be the priests over your homes. We need you to step up to the plate and be Godly men. Be led by the Holy Spirit. Then, and only then, can you truly love us as you should.

Now, there are some women out there that have the wrong

idea about marriage. Men don't want or need a gold digger. If you're a woman looking for a meal ticket or someone to make love to you when you want it with no guilt, then you're definitely not ready for marriage. Reminder—it's a partnership.

You know when you have a match made in heaven. It shows in the way you treat each other.

Again God tells me that I've suffered much in Minden. He tells me that I had gone through much and understood so little of it until later. He says, "I know your hearts desire is to serve me and others and that time is rapidly approaching. I sent you to the churches I wanted you to go to. The hurts in Minden are great. I knew they would be. It is time for you to live. You have taken care of my business and now it's time I take care of yours."

I failed to include this earlier so I will do so now. For years I had wanted the property adjacent to the house. It is a relatively large lot. Every since I first purchased the house in 1982, I had wanted that property. Well, the Lord led me to walk over it a few times and pray over it. I did. The last time I walked it He said praise Me for it. I did. I purchased that property at a price I could easily afford.

It was all grown up, covered with trees and all kinds of stuff. To show my appreciation to God for blessing me with it, I gladly got out there cutting trees, moving limbs, mowing—you name it, I did it. There were several people that helped to clear it. Initially it was me, Nikki and my neighbor, Ms. Claudie.

Where the property was located, people would often pass through and see me hauling tree limbs or branches, or clearing it one way or another. One man told me or rather asked me, "Regina, have you forgotten you're a lady?" I had not; I just wanted God to know I took nothing for granted.

After purchasing the property, I ended up transferring the house and the property over to a business partner. We refinanced or rather he did in order to pursue "God's Storehouse" and used the money from the refinancing to do just that.

When I realized that people were not going to support this endeavor like I thought, I tried to get my job back with the Social Security Administration in Minden. They ignored me and my requests for employment and actually hired someone who had never been an employee with the Social Security Administration. Now, I had twenty years in at that time and tried the first year to return. People, if you think I'm lying, I have proof.

Each year from about 2001 until 2003, opportunities presented themselves for me to return to the Social Security Administration in California. I turned them all down until later. I was not ready to leave Louisiana. That was home.

Allow me to add that during this time the manager that had worked for the Social Security Administration during the time when I left had been promoted and moved out of the state. Ted Robinson was the manager when I was there and he was good. And, *he could sing*, another of my heroes.

I tried to get a job as a substitute teacher. Even after taking the tests, going through the orientation, and going to get fingerprinted, I never got called. Well, I did briefly before they contracted it out to a temporary agency. They could not fingerprint the women when we went to the Webster Parish School Board to have it done. We were told we would be contacted to do it later. It never came to pass.

I worked for Wal-Mart for a brief time. Soon after God told me to leave there. People mistakenly thought that I felt too good to accept certain jobs. I didn't. I tried to obtain employment at a hospital in Shreveport, a casino, and many other places. I took tests, passed them, and walked away feeling pretty *"doggone"* good. I felt as though I had those jobs, only not be called back.

You might ask, how could they call me when my phone was on and off all the time? That was easy. I would leave my brother's and aunt's numbers and their phones were always on.

I ended up applying for food stamps. Thank God for food stamps. My family and I didn't go hungry. All I had to do was leave. Why did I stay so long? Pops was still there and still in bad health. Apparently I had not suffered enough.

So, instead of leaving I stayed and I suffered. Then I decided I would continue to pursue "God's Storehouse". Let me say this, there were many times I prayed and asked God to please allow me to take care of this one or that one. He allowed me to and I paid the price. God has a permissive will and a perfect will. Many times because of my caretaker mentality, I went through things because I just didn't have sense enough to let go.

Someone there told me that I was the wrong person trying to do the right thing. I often heard from people if someone came from somewhere else and presented this people would readily support it. A prophet (visionary) is not without honor except where? Among his/her own.

I am not going to go through each and every year now but rather attempt to bring this chapter to a close. There were several losses in my family during this time; two aunts, a niece, cousins and friends. The losses occurred due to death and some due to separation. With each loss, the pain became unbearable. There were other losses as well; loss of my home, loss of self esteem, loss in the way of broken relationships, loss, and more loss.

I ended up losing my house. It had been refinanced and put into someone else's name as previously stated. I had no job and unable to pursue my place in ministry. It was lost after it was completely paid off. Since I had no job and had placed it in another's name, the bank could not legally give me any information on the business pertaining to the house. By the time I left Minden, the account was in serious trouble. I didn't fully realize this until after moving to California.

Upon learning of the condition of the house, I attempted to

refinance the balance owed. I now had returned to my good government job and had a means to repay the loan. They said no as my credit was messed up. Hey! Didn't it get messed up trying to help the city? I know it wasn't perfect before. All of us know that now but if I paid it off the first time and the balance was much more, what would make them think I wouldn't pay it off again? That was our home. We were robbed and no guns or weapons were used—just the power of the people in authority. Well, on second thought, that is a weapon—power.

      The balance that was owed on the house and land was about ten thousand dollars. At least I think it was. No amount of my asking, begging or pleading would change their minds—banks policies and procedures. Okay.

      You talk about someone being screwed up for years after that took place. Can you even begin to imagine the hurts and pains felt in losing your home? We had already been displaced on several occasions and found ourselves homeless by some definition.

      Trying to help others and not getting the help I needed, my daughter and I ended up estranged many times. Her grades fell at school. Her only enjoyment and way of escape was through band. She played the drums in band and loved them. Yet, she was often one place and I was another. Talk about being mad with God and the people. I was mad!

      To God Be the Glory, after leaving Minden, my daughter graduated in the top fifteen in her class. This was a graduating class of about three hundred and she received all kinds of awards.

      Prior to my coming to California, one of the reasons I stayed as long as I did was because each time I mentioned to her about coming, she told me in no uncertain terms that she did not want to come out here at all. Now, she loves it more than I do.

      Our relationship fell completely apart. She lived with my goddaughter, April for a long time. I cried. She got to where she didn't want to be with me. I cried. And, I felt guilty because I was the mother and I should have been able to provide for her and shield her from all these hurts. She was angry with me and I am so sure disappointed with God. I know this because during this period, she started writing poems. I would find them, read them and cry. I just couldn't draw the strength to leave. Pops and so many others needed me and I wanted to stay home. God allowed it.

This is a good point to remind people to be careful what you pray for. You just might get it. Pray God's perfect will be done. If you ask for anything else you just may not want it when you get it.

Where was Kendrick during all of this? I've made many references to Nikki but no mention really of Kendrick. Well, Kendrick was in and out of jail on several different charges. When I moved from California in 1994 back to Louisiana, Kendrick went there, befriended someone who shot and attempted to rob someone not long after our getting there. Kendrick was with him. He was around fourteen. He did not say anything about the crime until the police came about a year after it happened. His reason for not saying anything was because he was afraid.

When I met the young man, I would often tell Kendrick he needed to be more like him. He seemed to be so polite and overwhelmingly courteous. Kendrick said nothing but would roll his eyes each time, never saying a word. Be careful who you tell people to be like—looks can be deceiving.

Let me add that I don't believe this young man was a bad person, although I do believe he was very confused.

After Kendrick's first trip to Juvenile Detention, he seemed to have just given up. Despite how many times I told him not to believe the lies of the people and that he could be whatever he wanted and do whatever he wanted to do, the more he seemed to be attracted to those that stayed in trouble—other hurting young men in need of Godly guidance.

Kendrick got out and announced one day to me that he and Keisha Fuller were getting married. I said to them, you all have a case of the "don't got no's". I said, "Kendrick don't have no car, house, job, nothing and neither did Keisha". They were adamant. So, after saying what I had to say and realizing it was going to take place, I went about helping them to pull it together. Can I get real? *"Something"* came to me and said. "I am doing this and I want you to help them". This was at midnight and it was then I got up and helped them to pull it together.

After the wedding they stayed with me and with her grandparents for a while. Eventually from there they went to Ohio and stayed with her mother, then onto Shreveport with an aunt.

By the time my first granddaughter was born they had been a few places. After her birth, Kendrick went back to jail. He got out again and the second granddaughter was conceived. By the time she was born he was back in jail. Why am I telling you all of this? There's a reason and a lesson for someone.

First off, I believe a Godly man should have a place for his new wife to live, some stability. Secondly, a Godly man should be able to provide for his wife. They were not ready as evidenced by all the ups and downs that have taken place from the very beginning.

I ended up from time to time having to spend nights with Keisha. She was there for me many times and I was there for her. When we actually started working on God's Storehouse, Keisha was running around with me. She was committed.

She and my cousin Shie went to training classes and helped others. Keisha did more paper work than anyone other than Nikki and I. Shie provided housing for Nikki and me for seven months but the majority of the actual work was done by Keisha, Nikki and I.

Now, with my son, I never adopted him or had legal custody in any way. I could not sign for him to get a drivers license. Yet, when the case went to trial it was determined that I was legally responsible financially for the victim's medical bills, loss of wages, etc. to the tune of numbers that would buy a house in California. I had no job. I had no income or means of paying this. But, wait? The judge said they had never had a case like that and did not have a precedent so how could I be found liable? I guess his case established precedent.

January 23, 2000

There are so many things happening now. All throughout this period I sent letters to any and everyone trying to explain the vision and trying to get support. They mostly continued to go unanswered.

The land next door is almost cleared. We have worked our butts off and really had fun doing it. I never realized mowing, cutting trees and doing lawn work could be so relaxing and therapeutic.

The City is installing a street light and old cars that have been located behind the property are being removed. Yes!

January 30, 2000

I need a job. Letters were sent to The Social Security Administration again in Minden and Willis-Knighton Hospital. I pray that some doors will open.

February 3, 2000

Where am I today? Thinking. It is really amazing to me that a person cannot receive a gift from someone without their thinking that there is some hidden agenda behind the gift. I have offered many things to many people and laid all of my cards on the table, so to speak. There are no secrets.

I've received many gifts from men that I was never physically involved with and I graciously accepted them. I've thought this entire time that I am really a strange person and I guess I am; strange in the fact that I really do care about and love people. I may dislike some of the things that people do but that doesn't stop me from loving the person. God has continually blessed me in so many ways that I want to share the blessings with whomever, whenever and however I can.

I have been off work now for almost a year and I've suffered some, however the sufferings are nothing compared to the blessings I continually receive. I have given so much to many others and now because of my giving doors were being opened for me to receive (Not from the ones I gave to). When we give to others that person(s) may never, ever give us anything back. God will use someone to help us in our times of need. The word says, "When we give to the poor we lendeth to the Lord".

When one meets the needs of others, God meets our needs. That is a fact. Sometimes things are delayed but definitely not denied. Patience, faith, prayer, belief, hopes in God and ourselves is the key ingredients for success. One's measure of success may not be the same as another. Success to me is having God as the head of my life, having a good family life, my needs being met and the means of helping to meet the needs of others. It is not about material things as they don't bring you peace of mind. It is not about money although it does take money to make things happen.

As Christians, once we realize that by daily surrendering our will to His will and daily inviting the Holy Spirit in to lead, guide and direct us, we will walk out our predestined purpose. Then and only then will we be able to enjoy where we are en route to where we're going. Only then will we be able to press on in the midst of all the storms and attacks by Satan when we hit those "stuck in the middle" or "in the meantime" states.

Don't think I've gotten it together now when you read all of this. Realize the full revelation and understanding comes many years later. Merely taking bits and pieces from my daily writings to pull this together is what I'm doing. Keep reading you will see based on subsequent days, months and years how I "*yo-yoed*".

February 10, 2000

My relationship with someone I considered a very dear friend has changed. I keep hearing in my spirit that this person has betrayed me. My phone calls go unanswered and no return calls are given when I've left numerous messages. What did I do?

It's the people that are the closet to you that will hurt you the most. Everywhere we are in life is exactly where we're supposed to be; at least that's my belief. People are at different levels spiritually, educationally and in so many other ways. Sometimes God tells us to back off from people as He is doing a work in that person's life. Maybe this is what's happening here with this relationship. At any rate, it still hurts.

February 16, 2000

I'm in serious debt again. Every time I have believed I was coming completely out of debt I've ended up either making new bills or having to maintain the regular bills at the house. I've heard Keith Butler and Joyce Meyer both mention how they were led to leave their jobs and the struggles they went through. It doesn't make it any easier knowing that others have struggled too in pursuit of ministry.

With the help of Pastor Clarence Calvin and his wife, Sandra, my family members and I formally established the name "God's Storehouse" in 2000. We obtained our 501(c) 3, non profit status, obtained the business license through the City of Minden and set about doing many good works in the City.

Initially, we were under the umbrella of Liberty Christian Ministries. Pastor Calvin helped us to develop a mission statement, strategic plan and set forth action steps to make the vision become a reality.

On paper, the first members were Rev. Robert White as Executive Director. I along with Della Mixon was the other Associate Directors. The Board of Directors consisted of Dierdre Richardson, Leroy Jones, and Byron Marcel. Our mission was to holistically meet the social and spiritual needs of those in our community or to connect them with resources that could.

We provided Emergency Services by giving furniture, dishes, pots and pans and the likes at no charge to people financially unable to obtain otherwise. Mostly all of the donations of these items came from family members in one way or another. We provided Technical Assistance on matters ranging from *A* to *Z* according to our levels of expertise.

The organization became members of the Homeless Organizations Providing Empowerment (HOPE) formerly NW Louisiana Homeless Coalition); Service Connection (formerly Shreveport-Bossier Service Connection); members of the Minden-South Webster Chamber of Commerce. We recruited people and some of us ourselves worked with the building of Habitat homes.

The organization provided Information & Referral Services for those in need, sending many letters of referrals to various agencies when contacted by clients to help meet the need in that person's life.

The organization participated in a food distribution working with *Feed the Children* during the Thanksgiving holidays donating boxes of food to those in need.

We sponsored a walk team for a couple of years with the *March of Dimes* and we did all of this with very little support of those within the community we strived to serve. Pledges were made but the money to cover these usually came from my own pocket.

Linked with Service Connection afforded us the opportunity to link by computer with mostly all of the helps ministries in the NW

Louisiana area to meet the needs of those who contacted us.

Our goal was to serve all of Webster, Claiborne and Bienville Parishes. We ended up assisting people from other parishes as well as the needs arose.

Our slogans were… "Help Us to Help You", "Family Taking Care of Family" and "Together We Can Make It Happen". "God's Storehouse", where families can pray together, work together, learns together, grow together and prosper together based on the premise that we are all family.

The structure changed after a few years and I became the Executive Director and the Board of Directors changed. We knew that we needed a diverse group to sit on the Board to ensure the needs of the community were being addressed and not the needs of any one family or one particular group. Several times extended letters were sent to various ones within the community asking, begging, and pleading for others to come on board. We needed to have a legitimate organization in the real sense. The letters went unanswered and ignored.

Letters were extended to business people, ministers, and lay people to come on board. Mr. John Dixon, Minister Mary Ferrell Colquitt, and Attorney Marcus Patillo answered the call. Thanks to all of you. By then apparently the damage had been done. The people still would not support us.

Ronnie Vietch answered the call and supported us many times as with the Coca Cola Bottling Company. A few of the stores assisted us with donated items when we attempted fund-raisers. Thanks to Save-A-Lot, Minden Market and OJ's Super Foods.

In the parable in Matthew 20:1-16 where Jesus closes with "the last shall be first and the first shall be last; for many are called and few are chosen", it talks about how hired men that came in at the eleventh hour still received the same pay as those who started out at the beginning. The people thought it unfair because they had worked longer hours and yet the ones who came in later received the same pay. The moral of this is it doesn't matter when people come on board, the pay is the same.

In Matthew 24, The Wedding Feast, another parable was given. In this one a king invited people to a wedding feast for his son. He sent out invitations to the prominent ones (and I am paraphrasing) and they didn't come. He did the same thing a second time and got

the same results. Then, what did the king do? He had his servants go into the highways and byways and invite people to come and they came. That's what I did.

Another thing that really took place during the breaking period is my writing of love letters to God on a regular basis, at least once a week. It was awesome writing a letter to Him, wait and work and then He would tell me of His love or plans for me. Awesome!

March 26, 2000

Pastor Calvin told me some things that puzzled me. He said, You cannot continue to wait on people. You cannot share your dream and vision with everyone. People will take it and run with it. It seems like you are trying to stick with what is familiar". My understanding of what he was saying came later.

We wanted to get the word out that disaster can strike anyone at any time and we should be prepared when it does… ignored. We tried to encourage people to educate themselves, to read, to never give up. We tried to encourage in every way possible.

May 24, 2000

It's Wednesday and all day yesterday I hear, "Today marks the end—the end of your chasing Robert (Yes, I did chase him and letters sent—oh my God, it seemed to have been hundreds), the end of your being broke, the end of your trying to have things your way. This is the end. Now, let Robert chase you if he wants you. You are about to meet someone and you will date that person—God's way. He will be interested in you and you in him. You will very soon meet your real husband or the one I have for you. I presented you and Robert to each other. You were obedient and chose Robert. Robert still does not choose you. Forget about Robert now and move on."

May 25, 2000

It is a good idea for people to get the entire family involved in issues pertaining to goals—short and long term goals. Write that vision on the table and make it plain. It is also a good idea to involve the family in issues pertaining to finances, education, church, etc.

We, as parents, want to give our children the world when it comes to material things. Let's give them the world in reference to what matters most—our love and our time. Let's strive as parents to teach our children to trust in God, to develop a relationship with God, to pursue their purpose, to become self-sufficient and to teach others how to do so. That's what lasts and changes generational curses to generational blessings.

Giving them the newest sneakers or things we cannot afford does nothing but give them a false sense of what's important. Trying to keep up with the Jones is crazy. Who are the Jones' anyway? Do they really have money to buy or afford what they purchase or are they merely another family knee deep in debt?

The scripture does state if we delight ourselves in the Lord, He will give us the desires of our hearts. He will. Some things we desire are not good for us and some things our children desire are not good for them.

Each and every day we live and learn. Life is a journey. We move daily towards a destination that we may or may not even reach in this lifetime. If we train our young in the right way we will leave a lasting legacy.

June 20, 2000

It's Tuesday and I hear, "Give Robert (which one?) half of what you get today. You are about to get a lot of money and give Robert half for bills". I also hear that Robert will come running over here very soon to get me.

"Robert needs money and wants money but more importantly Robert needs and wants you. Robert knows this and has for a long time. Robert is now afraid that he is losing you and Robert will not have that. Robert doesn't give a darn about your house but he does give a darn about you. You are a goldmine and one anyone in their right mind would want. You have gone to bat for Robert and Robert has done nothing.

Robert knows beyond a shadow of a doubt that you truly love him for him. Turn around Regina, turn around. It's your time for your thing from your God. I have all power and I am now going to show it to you. You have been lied on, cheated, talked about and mistreated and you have stood. You are now ready to do the works that I have for you to do. Until you had gone through all of this, you were not ready. You are now.

Robert is just as ready as you are. Robert wants to marry you and now is as good of time as any. Robert never, ever wants to lose you—not now, not ever.

Regina, open the door for your husband and give him everything in this life that he needs and wants. Robert will do the same for you. It's not a game. This game ended and Robert is coming to turn this house into a home.

Regina, don't worry about money or anything else. The way has already been made. Your windows of blessings are opening now.

Rejoice and praise me. Do not worry about anything at all. Robert, your hero, your lover for life is coming for you.

Robert is your ministry. You and Robert will handle my business first and I am going to bless the two of you abundantly.

The best way to get revenge on anyone is to forgive. You have forgiven people but forgiving does not mean going back. Get ready Regina to receive your blessings…all of them."

Okay, so we're back to Robert again. Will I ever be able to get away from him or rather them?

June 21, 2000

Today is Nikki's birthday. Happy Birthday Nikki! I wrote her a special note. She is a great young lady and my very own special gift from God.

Her note went like this:

> *"I'll get you a card but no card can say how proud I am to be your mother and have you as my daughter. Children are a gift from God and I thank Him daily for you. You are warm, loving, kind, compassionate, and very gifted and talented. You are a carbon copy of me." "You don't complain and realize how blessed you are. Who wouldn't want a daughter like you? Only a foolish person would not. As you enter your teen years, always remember that you are first and foremost a mighty young lady of God. Dare to dream. Know that the sky is the limit and with God you cannot fail.*
>
> *Trust Him. Believe Him. Believe in yourself and you will go far. Know this, God loves you and so*

do I. I thank Him for a wonderful daughter and friend in you. Your Mom."

Let me right a wrong that I stated earlier, Minden, Louisiana has a bunch of giving people as evidenced by the Saint Jude donations each year as well as many other significant contributions to various ministries. There are many people there who truly do care about others and want to make a difference. Sometimes, I believe, many give to the point to where they feel taken advantage of. We, "God's Storehouse" are stressing giving people what they need as opposed to what they want so that our giving is not in vain and we are not taken advantage of.

There are some vicious people in Minden. There are some everywhere. There are a lot of Christians in Minden as well though.

June 28, 2000

Nowhere in the Bible does it state that Christians cannot have fun. At least no where that I have seen. There are ways that do not interfere at all or compromise us at all in our beliefs as Christians. Couples and people in general can and should come together for fun times, regular Bible studies, and to socialize. There should be daily prayer time. But what about doing some fun things, having some balance?

There are too many sour faced Christians walking around for me. Lighten up! Keep it real! Have some fun! Who would want to serve a God that required we walk around looking like we sucked on prunes all the time? Who would want to serve a God that required we were serious all the time? How can we draw others to Christ when we look and act like that all the time? We can't. Instead of running to us they run away from us.

I had to learn that God is a good Father and He wants me to

enjoy life and you too. I absolutely cannot be anyone but me. Others may find me hard to take but I'm best at being me and so are you. God knows who each and every one of us is. When He made each of us He threw away the mold and said it is finished. Everything He made was good so why try to change and be someone you're not.

If you're normally a serious person by nature then that's who you are, accept it. That's just not me and I accept it.

Okay, let's talk about a very controversial issue—women in ministry. Listening to the radio station this morning there was a debate going over this issue. Someone said that we as Christians are all called to ministry. A lot of people disagreed over a woman in a pastoral position. One caller stated that Satan is causing the confusion over this issue as he knows this is his last chance and we should not be concerned as to who is giving the word but more so concerned with kingdom building and soul winning.

My sentiments exactly. What difference does it make who gives the word and in what capacity? God can use anyone He wants in anyway He wants. And, no I will not debate the issue. That's for God to do with people not me.

The Word of God gives us the great commission—"Go ye therefore and teach all nations". Get on God's agenda people. It doesn't say man go or woman go, it just says "go". Stop bickering over who you think is called or qualified and who's not. Don't try to be God Jr. He doesn't need our help in that area.

Know where and what position you are called and chosen to do and then do it. I know my calling and the devil in hell cannot take that away. He tries to stop us but he can't unless we let him.

Who am I? A prophetess, teacher, singer, writer, motivational speaker, business woman, a mother and mainly a help-mate to my husband when the time comes. I am an encourager and a giver. What or Who qualifies me? God. I've often heard it said He doesn't call the qualified, He qualifies the called. It's not debatable, at least not with me.

God said to me during this same month that He did not break any down as He did with me and that He is not going to build any up with me. He said it.

July 18, 2000

God said to me on this day that Annette would take my position. I thought He meant Annette Jefferson but it ended up being Annette Jones Davidson some years later. You know I told Annette Jefferson it was her and she repeatedly told me that it was not. Okay, remember now people, God did tell me a few pages back and some years ago that other people would do things than those originally given. He said, I thought and was wrong most of the time.

July 27, 2000

I hear that I am about to get an obscene amount of money, really obscene. Bring it on! I'm broke. Well, you know it didn't happen, at least not yet. And maybe not until after this book is completed. There I go guessing again. Remember the scene from Pretty Woman?

August 11, 2000

6:25 p.m. "The deal that you and Robert will close on Thursday will not be a monetary deal but rather a marriage between the two of you. Thursday is the day that you and Robert become husband and wife. On Sunday Robert will propose and the following Thursday, you and Robert will be married." That's what I hear.

August 14, 2000

On this day I heard that both the Social Security Administration and another place in Louisiana will contact me about a job, but I will not take them. Instead I will rather work side by side with my husband in "God's Storehouse" and his business.

August 15, 2000

This evening God said to me that I am still wrong about some things. He said that the breakings ended a while ago, the surrendering and accepting Robert took place Sunday.

He also said it was not me alone who had kept this vision from manifesting as it never was about me. God said, "Regina, you have been obedient all the way. This is about a coming together of people."

I have had my hands on every aspect of this ministry assisting others while trying to beg, plead and plod people into action. I've hand my hands on when many times I needed more than anything to have my hands up.

There were many people waiting and hoping to see what I could do for them. That appears to be the case. When we, being my family members and a few others, really came together, we were able to do a strategic plan and develop action steps. All hell broke loose not long afterwards and that was the end of "we".

In the meantime I have been continuously running around here networking, learning any and everything I can that pertain to many different issues. Many people have similar dreams and visions. Many times it's the coming together that makes them happen.

Networking is so important. It is humanly impossible to know everything about everything and we shouldn't even try. Many times I've said to people that I'm not the smartest person in the world by any means but as long as I know who to go to get the answers I need that's all that matters. God gives us a lot of resources through each other.

    This has been said many times in the writings and bears repeating again…God can use anyone in any way He wants to bless us and Satan will use anyone in any way to delay the blessings God has for us. Lesson—Know who's pulling your strings.

Thursday, August 17, 2000

Dear God, My Wonderful, Loving Father,

*   Lord, I want to thank you for your goodness. I want to thank you for making ways out of no way. I want to thank you for loving me and so many others enough to break us to the point of our surrendering totally and completely to You. I just want to thank you today.*

*   Father, look upon our city, PLEASE and return us all to stand right with you. Forgive us all Lord. We need it. Clean us all up so that we can start afresh.*

*   You chose each and every one of us to do a job for you. I have not been slothful nor have I been disobedient, at least I don't believe I have. I have gotten so very tired to the point that without a miracle today I cannot make it. I need a miracle, a boost. You decide what that will be. You know what I need.*

*   I have poured my heart out to you over and over again. I have cried and cried for the people. I have moaned and moaned for the people. God, I need the people to do something for me now.*

*   Some have not surrendered their will to Your*

will yet. Surrendering is hard sometimes, probably most of the time.

As I go this morning to meet Pastor Calvin, I am praying that when I see him face to face, I will have money to give him. Nevertheless, not my will but Yours be done. I pray this is your will as well.

Please silence the attacks of the enemy in our city. Father, it is You and You alone who can do this. I can't but You can.

I thank you God for hearing my prayers and God thank you for watching over my children and each and every family member I have, which are many.

At this point, the only true friend I have is You. We are the only ones who have established a real covenant agreement. No others have done so. I pray that changes.

Your humble servant,
Regina G. Mixon

Today I typed the letter of termination ending the Memorandum of Understanding (MOU) between Liberty Christian Ministries and God's Storehouse. I didn't want to but felt I needed to. Pastor Calvin reluctantly took the letter. He stated that he believed this was for me to look over a year from now and laugh. I honestly don't believe that to be the case.

Elder Mason with Temple of Deliverance in Shreveport told me a while ago that God had told him to tell me to get my papers in order and once that's done the ministry will take off. Which papers?

I hear later to get ready for some changes. I also hear to not be so sure about some things or rather some people. I hear that some people will actually have a change of heart and some people will be replaced by others because of their disobedience. God says some people are not going to come back in my life not now, not ever.

He says that I can get another job, get another house but I cannot go forward with the writings of this book without Robert. Remember, there have been many of them and each has played a significant role in my going to the next level. They each came at various times throughout these years but each helped in some way or another in a big way.

Tuesday, August 29, 2000

"Regina, go to church and allow me to bring everything to you that you need. Robert will have one last chance to right his wrongs. His decision this time will be the final one. Leave Robert alone now totally and completely. If he should decide he wants to talk to you, let him come to you.

I have given Robert many opportunities to right his wrongs. I am not going to allow Robert or anyone else to hold up the blessings I have for you. You need them now and this is the time when you'll get them. Not tomorrow, but now.

You, Regina, have gone through much and so has Nikki. Nikki wants and needs things. She deserves them. I am a good Father and gracious and loving and kind. I whipped you in line with my will for your life and now I am about to give others some royal whippings.

My word says, "Touch not mine anointed nor do my prophet no harm. I sent you to the people with a word from me. When they rejected you, they were actually rejecting me. Vengeance is mine and I am now about to repay. Be still and know that I am now fighting this battle.

You don't have to cry anymore. You don't have to or need to worry about anything. Watch My power! I am having those same people who have misused and abused and rejected you, come to you and right their wrongs now.

Regina, you have waited on me. I have waited on the people to do the right thing. I, like you, have gotten fed up with the people of the City and Regina, they are now about to see my wrath. There is about to be a real shaking going on.

One in particular is about to see my wrath. How dare he believe or think it is My will for him to live a sinful life-style as he has and to give my word. I am going to whip some people in line, starting with the preachers.

The preachers will come to you. Don't worry about Pastor Calvin or any of your bills. The way has already been made for you.

I know that you think you are a nobody; but you are not. You are one of My own chosen ones, hand picked to do a job that you are well able to and will carry out.

Rest today. Just simply rest today and wait this day on me. What has been impossible for you to do; I will do. Watch My power.

Today ends it and August is your month. You, Shie and Nikki all go to church. Don't focus on the negatives. Have praise parties and leave these men alone. I am about to handle them in a way that they will come running here begging the two of you. Get ready."

Friday, August 25, 2000, 4:35 PM

My lights and gas are still on. *TO GOD BE THE GLORY!* Why am I saying this? I'm past due on each of these and have no money to pay them. Most people don't know I am still writing on this book. I'm sure if some knew they would not even talk to me. They think it's a game. It's not.

I have done some things in pursuing this vision and dream that have even shocked me, things that I would never, ever normally do. I have exercised ridiculous faith believing that God is going to give me some ridiculous blessings.

Nikki was upset as we had gone two places trying to sell her drum set to get a marching snare that she needed for school and neither would accept them. I told her I believe God is trying to give her something in addition to what she already has. She's okay for the time being.

Right now I really and truly feel sorry for the many people I have bugged during this waiting period. All were done by the leading

of the Holy Spirit but still my heart does go out to them.

God is good! Ronnie Veitch sent a fifty dollars donation today. God knew we needed it.

Monday, August 28, 2000

Pride, fear of failure and selfishness are things that hinder change from occurring in our lives. I ask myself this morning, do I have any pride? Well, exactly what is pride? It's exalting our accomplishments above others and to be arrogant and excessive in self esteem. It can be so much more as well.

Today I am taking inventory of myself as it is much needed. I'm examining myself according to the scriptures. I am being brutally honest with myself. Do I like what I see? No.

I do not believe that there is any spirit of pride. I do not believe that there is one shred of selfishness. I do believe that there is a certain element of fear.

I am neither arrogant nor excessive in self esteem. If anything, my self esteem has been torn down completely. There are no major accomplishments to exalt above others, none at all.

I have learned some very valuable lessons the hard way. God has given revelations in some areas pertaining to life but He has graciously done this with, and for, most Christians or those who are receptive. I am thankful for that He has given me.

Where does the fear come in and can it be hindering my succeeding in reference to this ministry and life in general? The fear comes in not knowing how certain things are going to be done. It comes in not knowing how bills will be paid. It comes in knowing that there is so much negative talk and people are waiting and watching. It comes because of people's judgments of me.

Fear is of Satan and God has not given us a spirit of fear. The reality for me today is there is so much fear. One cannot operate faith and fear at the same time. We must choose. The Bible states we walk by faith and not by sight. It also states the just shall live by faith. It's a choice.

I know I need to exercise more faith. I also know that living solely by faith as I have done for the past year or so have exhausted me to the point that I know nothing now.

The wonderings and wanderings have kept me from walking into the Promised Land. There is nothing in this world that I would rather do than pursue this ministry and obtain all of the promises God has for me—nothing.

God said for me to take care of His business first and watch Him bless mine. I am not so concerned at this point about my business being blessed. I am concerned about taking care of God's business.

Only God knows for sure what the divine plan is. Know this much, my life is still so out of order and messed up that only He can restore.

At this point am I running away from things instead of facing them head on? Yes. Why am I running? I don't know what to do.

In the same interview I referred to a few days ago that dealt with women in the ministry, a woman minister said when God called her for about a year or so she was unable to attend hardly any churches and it hurt so bad. She said, "Lord, you've called me to the ministry and I don't understand what's happening." Well, the same here.

God loves a cheerful giver, not grudgingly or of necessity.

The giving I have been doing lately has had very little cheerfulness attached to it.

Nikki has said that she does not want to live in California and she has made that quite clear. I let go of the dream believing that like Abraham with Isaac, by letting go, God would give it all back to me. It hasn't happened yet.

I used to be in church every Sunday, Wednesday and all throughout the week during revivals at different places. Now, I am

hardly in church at all. That is what bothers me more than anything. My grandmother made sure that we went to church. I grew up in church. I strayed some when I got older but for the most part, even in my most sinful states, I went to church. I love it and I love singing, praising and serving God as best as I can.

So what is really my problem today? My walk is not lining up with my talk. God is pleased when they're in line. How do I get them lined up? I don't have a clue.

What is my first step? Prayer for understanding and guidance. What next? Obedience to the leadings of the Holy Spirit. What else? I really don't know.

God has proven Himself countless times in my life. God knows what I need and He knows what I want. I want a church home, a paying job, to go forward in this ministry, my family back and my house turned into a home. I also want a loving, Spirit filled, anointed man of God as a spouse; someone I don't have to beg or plead with to take care of God's business all the way, the right way and real, true Christian friends. Is this too much to ask for?

The voices I hear now I believe are mostly those of Satan. I don't know. This much I do know, "It is time for me to get back to work on cleaning this property". Right now I am going to do everything I can to pursue this ministry even if it's inch by inch.

Friday, September 1, 2000

The lights are off, it's midnight and I am home alone. They were shut off yesterday. Nikki and all of our frozen foods are at a family member's house. It's hot and I have many candles burning. I write now by candlelight.

Monday, September 4, 2000

Today in the mail I received information from the Foundation for the Mid South. I distributed the information to some of the area churches as I was led to do. They provide grants and other assistance for non-profits.

A day or so ago, a lady donated a portable building to the ministry. Thanks, Mrs. Woodard.

Questions again—

- ❖ Who do I love the most?
    - *"God, family & the church"*
- ❖ Who has hurt me the most?
    - *"All of the above"*
- ❖ Am I bitter or upset?
    - *"No"*
- ❖ Am I angry?
    - *"No"*
- ❖ Am I hurt?
    - *Not anymore*
- ❖ Am I harboring any resentment?
    - *"No"*

- ❖ Have I forgiven all?
  - *"Yes"*
- ❖ Have I forgiven myself?
  - *"Yes"*
- ❖ Will I help the people when they come in?
  - *"Yes"*
- ❖ Are there any at all I would not help?
  - *"No"*
- ❖ Even though they have not helped you Regina you are still willing to help them?
  - *"Yes"*
- ❖ Will I continue to give when I no longer need to?
  - *"No"*
- ❖ By giving to others when you don't need to, what does it do for the receiver?
  - ***"It hinders their growth and delays their blessings".***
- ❖ What does it do for you?
  - *"The same"*
- ❖ Regina, if I sent the husband in that I have for you today, will you accept him?
  - *"Yes"*

September 9, 2000

You know, Minden is God's concern and not mine. I've taken on people and responsibilities that are too much for me. I cannot do one thing to change or improve anyone's circumstances. I can do something to change things for me and Nikki.

If God sees fit for me to stay here, He'll supply both money to pay my bills and a paying job now. He knows that these are needs. Didn't He say He would supply all of my needs? So, what's happening?

If He doesn't do it, then it's time to move on. The disappointment on my daughter's face, the hurts are just too much for me. It's time for me to wake up from this nightmare. The dream or nightmare, whatever you want to call it is over. I am sick of this.

There are some things I cannot change. I repeat the serenity prayer—God grant me the serenity to accept the things I cannot change, courage to change the things I can and the wisdom to know the difference. It's time to really love me and my kids.

September 11, 2000

The book ends now! The last two chapters have changed; at least I believe they have from what I originally thought they would be. I need to and have to be whole—nothing missing, nothing broken, to do God's will for my life and I am not. I have to have many things before anyone even listens to me.

God provides wisdom to all. The Word says that if any of us lack wisdom, let us ask God who gives to all men liberally. A wise person knows that one cannot live without finances.

Doors have opened for me to go to California again. No doors have opened still for me to stay in Louisiana. I've looked too long at closed doors.

My life will never be the same and I'm glad. I've gone through so much and today I make the decision to get off this roller coaster. The ride has been too bumpy for me.

It hurts having to let go of people I love. It hurts letting go of this house. It hurts letting go of "God's Storehouse". These hurts are real.

Now God speaks to my heart that no job or amount of money without the people is enough for me to stay in Minden. He says if Robert doesn't come for me today, I am free to shake the dust off my feet and leave Minden and not look back. He says it's time for Nikki and me to live."

Friday, September 15, 2000

I hear today that I am about to make Robert look real good. I also hear that I have told Robert over and over again of my love for him and now Robert will tell me and show me his love for me. I hear that Robert is in real trouble as he knows he has to come for me now.

I hear that Robert knows that I am the best thing that ever happened to him and that Robert will not want to date at all but get married. I hear that Robert does not want to and will not lose me.

I hear that Robert wants a trucking company but more importantly Robert wants me. I hear that Robert is bringing me fifteen hundred dollars. God says, "This is my promise to you."

He says for me to not worry about one thing but to continue to look to the hills from whence cometh my help, knowing my help comes from Him. He says He is sending me all the help I need.

He says that Robert and I will help each other to be the best each of us can be until death do us part. He says we will continue to teach each other and many others. Regina, He says, it's all for My glory. The book is ending.

Well, during this entire time the conversations that take place are mainly between God and me. Do I even talk to Robert much? No.

Oh, God spoke and said to give Him one week to put closure to this. He said this last week. All I can say is His weeks are the longest ones I've ever seen.

September 25th, 2000

I hear, "I asked you to give me until Thursday to put closure to this and you did. Now, I am asking you to give me until Wednesday to turn things around completely". (Which Wednesday?)

September 27th, 2000

"Regina, watch Me do today what has been impossible for you to do." I hear that I need to get dressed as Robert is coming for me today. I hear for me to sit still at home, give God one hour, and allow Him to bring the money to me. Okay

October 6, 2000

No lights again.

Saturday, October 27, 2000

Yesterday I strongly considered suicide. Then I thought what would happen to my children if I did this? Life has become more and more unbearable. I am not in any way living the life I dreamt of or even the old life I had. I am stuck in a place I absolutely hate…mentally, physically, spiritually and financially.

My kids are not with me. Nikki is mostly at my cousin's now. God knows I do thank Him for her.

I am honestly ashamed to go certain places. I owe some money and it's downright embarrassing not knowing how and when I'll be able to pay them. I want to do laundry, my hair and nails. I have no lights. I really don't understand what's going on.

Sunday, October 29, 2000

I continually hear that today some very bizarre changes are going to take place and that today will be a very unusual day for me. I hear that my family will now come together and stay together. I hear that people who had not been willing to help me in the past now are. I hear an awful lot.

Monday, November 6, 2000, 11:30 PM

"Regina, you, Shie and Nikki all need each other desperately now. All three of you need to look for ways you all can help each other. The three of you must now look at what each of you can do to help the other.

Nikki is hurting. So are you and Shie. All three of you have been life on, cheated, talked about and mistreated. All three of you have been misused and abused. No more Regina. You will find that together the three of you have more power than you think.

I told you in advance that you were going to lose some people. You assumed all would be to death and that it would be others than those in your own family. A male friend I connected you with is going to lose his physical life. I will not say who that person is. I will say it is not anyone in your immediate family.

Byron, Janet, and Leroy, will be paid much for their faithfulness. Janet nor Kinete nor Della will work for "God's Storehouse" once it's up and running. Neither will Bruce, Leroy or Dee Dee.

All of your family will come together soon. All of those mentioned above are going to go through a breaking process similar to yours and Shie's. You, Shie and Nikki will not be here to see theirs. It's time for you three to move.

Regina, I don't mention Kendrick very much because if Kendrick is not careful, he will spend more time in jail. This is not My will for him but boils down to his choices. You, Nikki and Shie come together and pray mightily for Kendrick.

Prayer does change things. I will not force My will on

anyone including Kendrick and Shie. Shie is ready to do the work now and do the right thing. Kendrick will be soon but not yet.

Regina, I want you to go away for a while. You need real rest and fun. You also need to be in church services now. Pray for strength as Robert is coming. What come with Robert's coming are more attacks and more persecutions. I am silencing the enemy.

My word says I will rebuke the devourer. You prayed and asked me to. I heard and answered the prayer. I have done as you asked.

It is finally over Regina. It's been a long time coming but tomorrow you can sing, "I Made It" and mean it.

I would not allow you to return the dresses, plates, napkins, rotel tomatoes, ring pillow, shawls, cake cutter or server as you'll need them. As it is, you are going to have to buy back <u>everything</u> you took back plus more.

Tomorrow is a very busy day for you, no raking of leaves or any of that but busy nevertheless. Rest tonight.

Good night Regina and I love you." I love you too God. "How well do I know this Regina, you have proven it over and over again. Good night and pleasant dreams."

The next day God told me, "The husband He has for me is all bark and no bite. He has been hurt terribly in the past and that he, like me and a lot of other folks, has loved and not received real love in return. He is ready for real love now".

He told me to be patient, loving, kind and understanding with him; to be gentle and that he is fragile. He said that this person went through the breaking with me so that he, too, could get to the Promised Land.

God said, "He has prayed for me many times and that he just didn't realize what he was asking for". He told me to love him unconditionally then welcome him with open arms.

Monday, November 13, 2000

Today is the first day of Thanksgiving celebration at Willis-Knighton Hospital and it is a day of thanksgiving for me. My lights, cable and phone bill were **all** paid today after being off for months. Who did it? GOD!!! Who did He use? Pops! Pops gave me sixteen hundred dollars today. "To God Be the Glory!

All throughout this period, Pops has been really sick, both he and Mrs. Cre. I've taken them back and forth to the doctors, stayed in the hospital with him when he had to be hospitalized, ran to the store for them and handled their bills as far as obtaining, writing and mailing money orders. I also went various places picking up prescriptions and making payments in person. Thank you God for the blessings.

Wednesday, November 15, 2000,

The following I hear, "Regina, isn't it a shame that I am not going to let you take that job at Wal-Mart. Actually, Regina this time it will be your husband who will not want you to work there and he will say so.

Regina, get ready to receive all of your blessings. Some are not going to understand the move you are about to make but so what, you are blessed and it is time for the world to know it. Regina, the time has finally come. It is the set time, the appointed time. Again, well done thy good and faithful servant. I love you Regina and I am now about to let the world know just how much I love you. Watch My power now."

Footnote: I saw Shie change in the writings from my cousin to my daughter-in-law and to my niece, Shyeta. He said some people would change and I saw this just as I saw other characters change from people I originally thought would do certain things. Does God or did God lie? No. He doesn't force His will on any and all can be replaced. Choices.

The following Sunday I hear that I am about to do something ridiculous in order to receive many ridiculous blessings. I've done so many so bring it on. The way I see it, one more won't hurt anything.

Tuesday, November 21, 2000

Today I go for orientation at Wal-Mart. Say what??? Yes, I do. On Friday, November 24, 2000, I woke up at 5:30 a.m. and I'm supposed to be at work at 5:45. I set the alarm the night before and still overslept. Why? The alarm didn't go off. I heard on Tuesday for me to leave the job at Wal-Mart and I didn't. I heard again on Wednesday and I didn't. Then last night I heard a voice that said, "If I wake you at five o'clock in the morning, you know the job is yours. If not, you will quit the job at Wal-Mart. It is not My will for you to work at Wal-Mart but to continue to handle My business as you have and to trust Me." Well, all I can say is what's been said before, "Knock me down and call me stupid"

How can anyone explain this? I'm unemployed or rather not gainfully employed, have many needs and "something" leads me away from a paying job. I definitely don't understand this. Neither does anyone else.

Tuesday, November 28, 2000

It's about 8:20 a.m. and I hear, "Regina, do you trust Me?" I answered "Yes" and then I hear that something really good is about to happen for me today and that I should be prepared for some unexpected blessings to come my way."

I hear that I told you a male friend of yours would do certain things and he will but I did not actually say he would get a chance to do all of these things. I hear it's time for me to let go of him for good now.

"People are going to talk and some are not going to understand what is going on but that's okay, the understanding will come later for them."

"Negative things will be said about you when you and Robert marry. Believe me Regina, there will be many negative things said but Regina, I am about to bless you pressed down, shaken together and running over. I will silence the negative talk."

"You are getting married much sooner than you think—much sooner. Robert is no fool and Robert knows that if you walk out of his life, he will loose the love of his life. Robert knows that you have been faithful to him and him only. Regina, what man doesn't want to know that there is someone who is faithful to them in spite of them? None, Regina".

What man wouldn't want someone who is not a *"fuddy duddy"* and knows how to enjoy life? Regina, you have not really seen yourself for what you are. You are anointed and very much real. Some find you a bit hard to take but nevertheless, you are real. Many admire you Regina for sticking so firmly to that which I have planted in you and your desire to help yourself and others and serve Me to the utmost. Many admire you and you have been watched by many there in the City of Minden and you have, unbeknown to you, encouraged many just by your ability to stick to this in spite of the attacks.

You are strange Regina and very much unique.

What man wouldn't want someone who knows their role in life and has their priorities straight? I say, "None in their right mind".

"Regina, your brother loves you very much. You two have had your falling outs and now all I want you all to do is show love to each other and do it My way—that's all.

All of your family members will get it together. Love, Regina, love the people My way", said the Lord.

You are all anointed and very much blessed.

Now is not the time for any falling outs but a time of coming together. I want you to know that Satan has operated in each and every one of your lives from time to time during this waiting period. Strife, confusion, anger, division—none of that is from Me. You know where you erred and so do others. Now is the time for you all to do something about it.

It is time for you to share information with the rest of your family. Plan a "To God be the Glory" celebration this weekend and watch me bring it to pass.

Regina, I love you. I love you all and now I want your entire family to shake the haters off and to uplift, encourage and motivate each and every person you come in contact with—ALL for My glory.

You have written enough. Just merely believe and receive your blessings—all of them."

Later I heard as I was sitting at the hospital, "Remember your visits here with Nosha. Remember the trips you made here with her. (Kenosha was my oldest daughter that died years ago). Remember Northwest Louisiana State School." I said that I didn't want to remember.

Later, I hear that I had already sacrificed one daughter and that I do not need to sacrifice another one. I hear for me to go home and get Nikki and spend time with her. I hear if I don't give up the cigarettes I will sacrifice Nikki's life unnecessarily. Wow! Ouch! Ouch! Ouch!

Lord, please help me to give them up. I cannot do it by myself. I've tried and tried. Please help me.

Saturday, January 13, 2001

I am supposed to be on bed rest for the next few weeks. Huh! I have too much work to do. I had terrible chest pains and spent a day and night at the hospital.

Okay, I hear that Kendrick is about to help me much and that Kendrick has just been waiting for an opportunity to help me. That must be coming much later as it has not happened as of the writings of this book. Oh, since some have changed, is Kendrick really Kendrick? We'll see.

Saturday, January 20, 2001

They buried James "Goo" Andy today. He was one of my biggest helpers and supporters and just a great person. He had some problems but he would help anybody. I can't believe he's gone.

I was talking with Shie and Nikki on yesterday and told them that the Holy Spirit had spoken to my spirit and told me to get ready to lose someone very close to me. I asked them both; who could it be as if they would know. I repeatedly heard this and I was so nervous. It was indescribable and unexplainable.

Well, we found my aunt this morning in her apartment. She had gone on to be with the Lord. Then I hear after we found her that I am going to lose yet another person before God calls Pops home. How much can one bear?

I hear that Dorothy will call me and tell me that my mother-in-law has died. I just hear absolutely too much now.

"O death where is thy sting?" I'll tell you one thing it really hurts. I don't believe we're ever fully prepared. Maybe I'm wrong.

I keep hearing that my week has ended. As stated before, this has been the longest week of my life.

Thursday, January 25, 2001

I hear that I have done what needed to be done and now I am in need of much rest. God spoke in my heart that if I did not slow down and get rest I would join my Aunt Nell and the others before it's time and He does not want that.

So people, until today I have not been able to say no, but now I know I must unless I am ready to go, and to all of you that may not understand the thing I'm about to do. I say God will show you soon enough and as of today I'm through

Nikki, you said to me that I always want the house to be spick and span. Now all I am saying to you & Kendrick is just do the best you can

I've neglected you both in so many ways. To the point where I've shed many tears. Now all I ask is you two give me a chance. To make amends and right wrongs that has been in arrears

Neither of you have to worry about me from this day forward anymore. "To God be the Glory" today it finally sunk in. That after God and me you two come first.

It is as it should be.

Tuesday, January 30, 2001

After taking Nikki to school and watching Trinity Broadcasting

Network, something came to mind. God, I believe was taking me away from Minden. He was reminding me of the losses in my family I was about to face. I would have lost my family if I left.

Later in January I start to hear again that the 19th is a very important day for me. I heard to circle the 19th a while ago on the calendar. I guess it was January 19th and the year is yet to be determined. What do I know? Nothing.

God did tell me that I would go away and learn more so that I could teach and spread His Word, so I guess I really am going somewhere.

Tuesday, February 13, 2001

I should now be in a hospital. I feel so bad and have for a long time. Why am I not there? Beats me. One thing I know is I would have to have a place for my kids to stay. I've got some family members who would care for them, but I'm really making excuses now.

Thinking again…I've loaned about ten thousand dollars out to different ones. When I've needed repayment, those same people would say to me that I needed to get a job. Hello. I need my money back.

I actually thought I was doing the right thing by loaning to folks in their time of need. Lessons learned the hard way. I will not go into any details on this except to say a fool and his money are soon parted from each other. Learn God's way of doing things.

Someone once told me when I asked for money to be loaned to me, "People don't like it when the only time they hear from someone it's during a time when they want money." Well that statement definitely didn't apply to me because I am the one who is constantly contacting people with letters, cards, and phone calls, whatever. I love staying in touch with family. They may not feel the same way but I believe in family.

I have given my money, talents and time and what I've gotten in return is spat in the face. I've given up everything.

Tuesday, February 20, 2001

I hear if people need and want my help to let them come to me. I'm assured they will. I also hear that both Reverend (Reverend who?) and Robert (Robert who?) will need and ask for my help.

Wednesday, February 21, 2001

This is what God said to me:

>Regina, you're not going to Robert's tonight
>As all you 2 would do is fuss and fight
>If Robert wants to talk to you
>Let him now ask and
>Come for you
>
>You don't need to do any tricks
>To get Robert to come here
>Believe me, Regina and this time it's real
>Your time is very near
>
>I'm sending something in the mail
>That's going to make that poor boy bale (who?)
>And run here as fast as fast can be
>
>Whatever you need from this point on
>Don't ask anyone but me

You said it is very hard for you to be still
But now, Regina I know you will
You see I have a surprise for you
You and Robert each will very soon say "I do"

You'd better hide the tapes to this book
And place them in safe keeping
Now many are going to try to look
And try to do some peeking

Folks are starting to believe right now
Some are breaking out in sweats
Don't even worry about the folks
Cause they'll get what they deserve to get

Regina, I searched high and low
For one of great faith in your city or town
And in my searching my eyes landed on you
Now, I'll show folks I'm not playing around

Shie (Keisha & Gail later) is so blessed
So is Nikki too
As they believed without seeing

Others needed to see to believe
And believe me they'll **now all see**

I have a special surprise for you
One beyond your wildest dreams
Someone is coming to your door
And presenting you with some rings

The things you thought you'd lost
Well, they're not actually gone
You see, I am God and I do not lie
And I do take care of my own

You've entered into an entirely new season
Now many will know the reason
You went through what you had to go through

I am about to bless you abundantly

Because of your faith and your real love for me
I love you Regina and I always will
I am God and I know trust you to just be still.

Sunday, February 25, 2001

What is empathy? It is the ability to feel someone else's pain. From the latter part of 1998 until now I have felt the pain of:

1) Preachers-trying to minister the word to others
2) Women leaders/teachers—the opposition & rejection faced
3) Men—the put downs and challenges they face
4) Children—the real need to have Godly parents and Christian friends
5) Addicts—I walked through this pain
6) Alcoholics—I lived through their pain
7) Prostitutes—I felt their pain
8) Rejection, shame & humiliation—I lived through that
9) People letting you down—I made it through that
10) Having no money—I made it through that
11) Family & friends walking away—I made it

12) Ignorance in so many areas—I've lived through & continue to. I also continue to learn daily.
13) Abandonment, loss of loved ones, molestation, physical, mental and emotional abuse—I made it through this
14) Almost homeless—I made it through this

With being able to empathize with other people, or rather having walked through the pains of many, there is no way I can ever look down on anyone. I actually *felt* the pain of others and it hurt like crazy. I know others are hurting as well. Knowing the call of God on my life and what He has allowed to take place let's me know that there is no situation too hard for Him to handle and no one is helpless or hopeless.

Regardless of the pains we experience, at some point we have to get over them and move forward. How many times should we forgive our brothers? You know the answer to that. It's in the word.

How often should we forgive ourselves? Well, let's see, the word of God says when we confess our sins He is faithful and just to forgive us of our sins and cleanse us from all unrighteousness. It also says that He will cast them as far as the east is from the west. So, if God forgives us when we confess our sins, we should also be able to forgive ourselves as often as He does.

The same questions that were asked of me on September 4, 2000 were asked to me again on this date. The answers still remained the same. Then on March 12, 2001, I hear that I can stop mentioning Robert to anyone and date whomever I desire to. I hear that Robert made his decision and now God has made His. I hear it is time I really live and enjoy my life.

United We Stand

September 11, 2001 was a wake up call
To people throughout the land
Maybe God is trying to tell us all
That divided we fall
But **United We Stand**

Since that date, many forgot the differences
As far as race, creed or color
People merely started to look at others
As just another sister or brother

Churches were packed for a while
All over the land
But apparently some have forgotten
That divided we fall
And **United We Stand**

Every day is a day of thanksgiving

A day of rejoicing
For being among the living
There are no big "*I's*" or little "*You's*"
As there is plenty of work
For each of us to do

There should be new meaning to life, of God & family
Instead of taking so much for granted
Realizing that one day people and things will no longer be

Never hesitate to do what you can

To lend a helping hand
Because folks, once more and again
Divided we fall
But **United We Stand**

To the people in our city, parish & state
You're great people, each and every one
We really need to work together more
As we all have races to run
No matter where we may roam
There is never, ever any place like home
And by each of us doing our part or what we can
We will stand tall as **United We Stand**

When all has been said and done
And battles are fought and victories won
Together we can and will accomplish
much for this great land
Because we will not fall
<u>We will</u> **Unite and Stand**

Friday, September 28, 2001

I am ready to go to California. My only regret is I have to leave my daughter behind. I'll miss her so much.

I have to now find a means of supporting myself and my family and getting our lives back on track. I have said and God knows it is no longer my desire to settle for the crumbs from the table. I want no more leftovers.

The joke is on the people. In all of this, God has just been setting me up for many blessings. One of the many problems I've had is trying to *convince* people to believe in me and what God has placed inside of me. I tried to get people to believe the word.

God said He fixed it where people will no longer be able to take advantage of me. He did—He has been working on me. I thought originally like many others think that I'm okay the way I am so what needs to be fixed. I realized later there was much.

Having prayed in the past many times asking God to make me different, I did not fully realize what I was asking for. He did but I definitely didn't mean it the way He did it.

Always having the burning desire or passion inside me to help others led me to pray some real, fervent prayers. I was pushy, arrogant at times; hurt most of the time, shocked a lot by the unbelief pertaining to nothing but the word of God, and angry much of the time but then I realized that I am and have been dealing with people just like me.

Growing, I've come to realize that many are at different levels spiritually. Knowing that all are human and hurt in some way or another propels me to continue uplifting and encouraging any I come in contact with. I just have to know when to shake the dust off my feet and move on. Plant a seed and someone else will water it.

Sometimes by holding on we hurt the person and ourselves. Letting go is not easy but necessary. Many times in order for a person to do the right thing they first have to believe they are losing something or someone.

Sunday, December 16, 2001

The things I've needed most from people were love, understanding, acceptance and their support. Everything that I have done for others or almost everything has been ministry in one way or another.

People believed that I've tried to take something away from

them when in all honesty I have tried to give some things to them. It has been said that I don't back and support any church. That's not true. I back and support all churches. How can I be in regular attendance at the churches if I'm considered the joke of the town and I get the messages from members of various churches as to what's being said. You know, a negative message travels much faster than a positive one.

When I have something someone needs and provide it, I'm the best ***but*** when I have a need and express it, I have been considered nothing more than a mere bum. Never got an invitation to a dinner or a party or even visits much unless there was a need in that person's life that they felt I could meet.

I first saw this next thing happen about twenty years or so ago and I was amazed. Maybe you've encountered it as well.

Have you ever had someone need your help, I mean really need your help and you provide the help needed ***and then*** they beg you more or less to not let anyone know they had to obtain help from you. Huh???

Let me give an example. Someone needed some papers completed and knew you were well able to complete them, so they asked you, yet because of the talk around town they really don't want to be connected with you so they ever so politely ask that you tell no one.

I believe in confidentiality and all and if the motives were right…Moving on.

Nikki, God's Greatest Gift to me

One of the happiest days of my life was when God gave you to me
And I try so hard daily for the entire world to see

Just how much I appreciate the gift He gave to me

Many times, I know I have let you down
Causing you pain, sadness and often to frown
I thank God daily for His gift of you
And because of you, I can never stay sad or blue

A daughter is a source of pride, especially one like you
There is nothing in this world that you could ever do
To make me stop loving or be ashamed of you
God knows and I pray that you do too

That this is very true

So, at Christmas time and every day of the year
I thank God for His gift of you
That is so precious and dear

You say that you want to make me proud
Well that's not hard to do
The way to make me the proudest the most
Is to just continue to be you

I don't need or want a gift under a tree
Know that I have the greatest gift already you see
I'll love you always no matter what you do
You see, God's greatest gift to me has been and will forever be
"YOU"!!!

Merry Christmas 2001
Your Mom

I have to give a special thank you to two of my Pastors in Minden who did believe, Pastor James Brown of Full Deliverance and Rev. Rodney Williams with King Solomon Baptist Church. Pastor Williams and his wife on two to three separate occasions came in and met needs that my family and I had without being asked. Both men were very encouraging. Bishop Brown would always say to me…" a prophet is not without honor except in his own country."

I was actually a member at King Solomon's for much longer than Full Deliverance. Both men are mighty men of God. When Trinity Broadcasting Network wasn't feeding me, which was happening almost on a daily basis, these men were. Thanks again.

I'm not going into any more of the daily writings. It is my belief that by now you too have come to the conclusion that I am totally insane. You probably think it's either schizophrenia or some other mental condition that causes one to hear voices.

You may even think that there is no way any of this could be true. Well, just ask the hundreds of people I told all throughout this process and I'm sure they'll tell you it's true. You do know that God shows us the end at the beginning don't you? You also know that when one is being prepared to minister to others, many times strange things take place. You are aware of the fact that God does speak to us, aren't you? You do know that Satan does as well, right?

Well, if you don't, I really challenge you to get into the word. Oh, and you do know our lives were predestined before we were even formed in our mother's wombs, don't you? It's in the word. It didn't take God by surprise, only me and others.

You know there was a character in the Bible that told his dream and because of it all kinds of negative things took place **BUT** at the set time, the appointed time it did come to pass. You know that God gives each of us many visions and dreams, things it would take us many lifetimes to accomplish and He more or less says…choose.

I challenge you to read the Bible. There's some really good stuff in there. Once you really read it you might not think these things to be so bizarre.

At this point I believe it is time for me to move to the next Chapter. Suffice it to say that from March 26, 1999 until September 2003, it was a season of God's continual speaking, lack in one way or another, my trying to persuade and convince people to believe in the vision and the promises God gave me, my trying to get God to make me normal again, my wrestling with God and breakings, on my part.

My Pops died in March of 2003. It was at that point that God finally released me to leave Minden and return to work for the Social Security Administration in September, 2003. I struggled with leaving what was familiar, but like Abraham I went and what I thought was going to be so terrible ended up being one of the best things that could have ever happened for me.

The breakings didn't end completely when I returned. It was at that point when God actually started doing some building. As of this date, I've been broken in reference to finances; I've been broken in reference to dealing with real men, yet I still have not been broken completely with the cigarettes and diet cokes. I expect to be before the book is published.

Now, having been given some insight or a little of it, we move on to the next Chapter. Just read and watch how God moves and set things in motion for His glory. God is awesome!

Making it for me into the next Chapter is enough to say, "To God be the Glory." about itself. Stop, get a glass of water, rest your eyes and then proceed when you're ready. I am so ready!!!

Chapter Five

The Big Day

The big day finally arrived. It was Thursday, September 25, 2003 when I loaded up the bus and moved to Los Angeles. There were some people really upset with me because I hardly told anyone that I was leaving. Heck, I kept going back and forth and only really decided at the last minute. I packed everything I was taking in a few hours.

En route to California, I met a lady that I am still to this day friends with. Who would have known that sitting next to someone on a bus would lead to a relationship that has lasted the entire time? And, she is a mighty prayer warrior. I found all of that out later.

Arriving in California on Saturday, September 27, 2003, I was picked up by my sister and cousin. Nikki stayed in Louisiana with April.

I began work with the Social Security Administration in the Torrance office on September 30th. Instead of feeling like a seasoned worker, I was nervous and felt like the new kid on the block. A lot had changed since I left four years ago. I tried to play it off like I knew what I was doing or at least remembered *something*. It's amazing how much one can forget when they don't use it. I couldn't play it too well. I was the new kid on the block.

Two others began the day that I did. They were young ladies and I do mean young. Heck, I'm forty six years old now. They were early twenties. It seemed that it was much easier for them to grasp the information than it was for me. Do I suffer from ***ADD*** too?

I am in for a life-style change. Going from running to slowing down to almost a snail's pace. What do I mean? My sister announced to me when I got to her home that they go to bed every night at eight o'clock. I'm used to being in Wal-Mart at 1:00 a.m. or 2:00 a.m. or some ungodly hour. I'm used to cleaning and ironing and doing all kinds of things at night. Culture shock!!! (She was serious too)

I'd lie in bed thinking many nights, "Why am I here? I'm not even sleepy." When in Rome you do as the Romans do. I cooked for holidays and on weekends, but my sister Dorothy, cooked everyday! I mean full seven course meals. A part of me thought I had died and gone to heaven until it took me forever to lose all of those unwanted pounds. That food was so good though.

I'm back on my job, making money and should be feeling pretty good, wouldn't you think? Think again. I missed home so much that every week I was on my way back. You know, God said I couldn't go forward looking back. Honestly none of us can. That didn't stop me.

It's close to Thanksgiving now and Nikki says she's coming for the holidays. I'm excited! When she arrives, she gets off the bus and says she's not going back, as there were just too many problems on that bus. They were a few hours late. I said, "To God be the Glory, my baby's here to stay".

We're still at Dorothy's, but I know it's time for us to start looking for our own place. A few months pass before we actually find our place. I or rather, we got the place without completing an application at all. It was God!

My landlady reminded me so much of an older aunt of mine. Now, you have to know that this aunt would visit from California and we thought we were in military school or something when she came. She could give some orders. That was just her way as she was really all bark and no bite. Nevertheless, my landlady reminded me of her and I immediately put up a wall.

She tried to be friendly and offer good sound advice on some things. I always saw my aunt when I talked to her. Instead of dealing with her on many issues, I just ignored her for the most part. That caused problems for both of us.

She absolutely loved Nikki and she would counsel her on how to get over on me. Hah! I don't think so. Well, maybe it did work for a while.

We ended up living at that particular spot for about a year. During this time I started to aggressively try to pay the old debts owed. I actually paid many people I didn't owe one cent to. I felt like so many had done stuff for me that I owed many. And I did, just not the ones I gave to first.

Backing up a bit, I came here with a few suitcases and nothing else. So did Nikki. Actually, Nikki had a couple of back packs. We had to rebuild from zero. We had no furniture so we were very blessed when Robbie, a.k.a Robert, sold us his living room set, bedroom sets, dishes, pots, pans, dining room set, china cabinets, TV...it was a blessing. I was able to split the payments in two. God is good!

My furniture and other things are all in Louisiana in storage at my brother's. I couldn't go get the stuff and we needed it now so God did what He said He would do—supplied our needs.

I had a Toyota that Pops had bought for me but it was left in Louisiana and we really needed transportation. My job was several miles away from where we lived; the same with Nikki's school. She's a Junior now!

A perfect stranger to me but someone my sister knew actually loaned me the money to put down on a car—fifteen hundred dollars. I couldn't get fifteen hundred dollars from people that knew me yet a stranger loaned me money. Of course, I paid her back. The remarkable thing is she had only known me a few months. Awesome God!

Nikki was very active and got into band and some other activities in school. Her grades improved. Her attitude improved and things went quite well most of the time. We were back together again and I should be really happy, shouldn't I? Well I'm not because even though we are physically living together I feel as if I've lost that mother-daughter bond and it seems that there is nothing I can do to get it back. Boy, do I try hard. We were more like strangers. There was so much that I didn't know about her.

I still say, "God said", "God showed" or "God led", but not to the degree that I did it before, just a few times everyday. Honestly, what do I think the problem is? I can't figure it out.

Kendrick, I might add is still incarcerated and I've not seen him for a while now. I do miss him very much. We have been communicating by phone and by mail. It's just my desire to see him. It's going to be awhile before that takes place, a few years to be exact.

Keisha and the kids come out and visit. They stay a short while and leave. DI comes and visits and we go see Fantasia. That girl is a hard core fan of Fantasia Barrino. I would have had to be on my death bed, no scratch that; I would have had to have actually died to have gotten out of going to that concert. Don't get me wrong, I really like Fantasia but she took it to another level.

She told me before we went that she was not only going to that concert but she was also taking a picture with Fantasia. She took the picture with her and many others of her up close and personal.

We did not get the tickets until the day before the concert. We got two tickets for forty nine dollars on Ebay. God is awesome! To top it off, we got floor seats, great seats, sitting next to people that had paid as much as one hundred fifty dollars a seat.

Trying to pay old bills, get reestablished, pay new bills, buy a car, finance a daughter in high school, sow seeds into ministries and give to others continually took a heavy toll on my finances. What budget? There was absolutely no way I could work a budget as there were so many needs and not enough money. I'm back at my old habits again—giving when I don't need to, not being a good manager of my money but doing the best I could with what I had.

Satan really turned up the heat many times. I got tickets…one for running a red light. I was turning right on red. That *"No right turn on red*" sign mysteriously appeared after I made the turn. It was not there before. I didn't see it. I also got another ticket for running a light that had a camera on it designed to catch law breakers like me. It took my picture. There is no way I can say that is was not me. Then I got a "*fix it*" ticket that ended up causing me several trips downtown, costing me more money and a suspended license. Now, you know I absolutely cannot afford any tickets. I don't know who they think I am. I can't pay them.

When I returned to the Social Security Administration, I was seriously in debt, I mean for real, for real. Trying to pay one old bill at a time and maintain luxuries like lights, gas, telephone, and cable…well, that was just too much for me. Bounced checks, overdraft, deadlines extended, some things temporarily shut off. I bet you thought after all I had gone through I would know better by now and you would be…wrong!

The door was open for me to purchase computers, electronics, and furniture items just by being an employee of the Social Security Administration and no credit check was required. I bought a big screen HDTV, several computers for different ones (I wanted people to have a computer and I knew some couldn't afford to get one themselves. Could I afford them? Nope but that didn't stop me.) I bought a total of seven computers, Was I concerned about the fact that by not waiting and doing it this way I was paying more for the items than if I had just waited, paid my regular bills, saved the money and bought the things outright? No indeed. Why wait? Haven't we done without long enough? Doesn't the word say we are blessed to be a blessing? I'm pretty doggone sure God wants me to do this. After all, haven't I always prayed and asked God to bless me so that I could be a blessing? I'm rolling now.

Please allow me to state here that in buying these items for people, I do believe each and every time I was led by God to do so. Believe me many times I did not want to. Tests are what I believe were taking place; tests to see if He could trust me to use the money He blessed me so that I could be a blessing to others.

We stayed at the four-plex for about a year. I look at an apartment in Torrance, tell the manager I want it, give notice on the place we're currently staying at and then start to weigh the options. I go back and forward over and over again. I'm actually in my mind holding on to this place and trying to move into the new place—double minded, unstable.

There was no real problem except the notice had been given and I had verbally told the manager I wanted the other place. Did I take her a deposit? Nope, I'm still undecided. What happens? It doesn't take a rocket scientist to figure this one out. I end up losing both places. Bummer.

My landlady repeatedly asked me if I was sure I wanted to move. She gave me many chances to say I had changed my mind. I was adamant. No, I wasn't. I was upset because there were some things that needed to be fixed around there and I had asked a few times and they didn't get done. Imagine my surprise when she tells me after I've given notice that she thought the people had come out and done the repairs. Oops!

You're probably thinking, "Regina, what about all those scriptures you quote? What happened to all the prayers? Don't you *always* say to people, "Wisdom is the principal thing, but in all your getting, receive understanding." To that I say, "I am still much better at giving advice than listening to my own".

It amazed me that there were so many Christians working in the Torrance office. What was even more amazing was the fact that when I walked back through those doors, dumb and all, I felt like I had made it back home. I felt like the prodigal daughter had returned.

The people who work for the Social Security Administration all have to be special people. Dealing with the clientele that we do on a daily basis requires one to first be potentially eligible for benefits themselves. Well, you know I qualify.

We would often talk among ourselves telling different stories pertaining to our own lives and realized we all had a lot in common—we were on the border of being classified as insane. Don't take offense Torrance, it's all true anyway.

Now to get back to being serious, I did feel like I was right at home and still do. Those are the best bunch of people to work with in the world. No one really looked at me strange as I went about with my daily conversations saying "God said" or "God showed me". No one on the job, isn't that something? There were still a few in church that did.

Please allow me to stress at this point that I have worked with a great group of people at *all* of the Social Security offices I've worked in Minden, Inglewood, Watts, Crenshaw and Torrance. I have met some of the best people ever in this agency from the highest positions to the lowest and all were great to work with. Torrance is just extra special though.

One lady asked me after I had been there for a while how long I had been away from the agency. When I told her four years, she said, "Wow, Jeff took a great leap of faith in hiring you back as so much has changed". Talk about a very humbling experience. He actually did.

I'm sure he received some opposition and probably a lot of flack from some in hiring me back. But needless to say, thanks is nothing for what he gave me. He gave me my life back and for that I am eternally grateful. I know God uses anyone in any way He so chooses to bless someone and he used Jeff many times to be a real blessing to me and mine.

Not too long after I returned to the Social Security Administration, maybe a year or so later, Gail Marie Hughes King joined us in the Torrance office as the Assistant District Manager. We had worked together some years ago in the Watts office. I was excited to see a familiar face. Later, I started to run from her like people did with me. She pushed and encouraged me like I had done to so many in Minden. I began to understand why people ran away from me.

I would say that I was going to do this, that or the other and her response was consistently the same, "You can do it" and like I would do, she proceeded to ask me on a daily basis (maybe an exaggeration) what I was doing to pursue whatever. If you should meet her, please don't discuss your ideas with her. If you know what's good for you, *run* and not walk to the nearest exit.

If I said I wanted to be a rocket scientist all Gail would ever say is go for it. I was just joking.

Nikki and I had gone to City of Refuge but never actually joined. Gail is a member of The Word of God Baptist Church and she invites us there. When I first entered the doors there, it was déjà vu, home again. It was a set up.

Pastor W. Terrell Snead, II had recently become the Pastor there. He, his wife and family are all so anointed. He preaches and teaches with such fervency and the messages are always right on the money. I joined the church. That was another set up.

I will talk a lot more about these two in the last chapter of this book. The only point I want to stress here is every bit of the things that took place, the people I met, the studies done, were all set ups to be blessed. Reality check, I am already blessed but for the *manifestations* of the blessings to take place. These people are all "can do" people. You know, like I can do all things through Christ who gives me strength.

Not long after being at The Word of God, I start to teach the Women's Sunday School Class. We did topical expository teaching. The classes were interesting and informative. Pastor also asks me about taking the leadership role with "Virtuous Women of The Word" which was and is the Women's Ministry at the church. I joined the choir. For those that know me, you know I love to sing. Not that I am great at it but my heart is most definitely in it. I dropped the ball on all of these. I just wasn't ready. I thought I was.

For a while, I bounced back and forth between City of Refuge and The Word of God. I just love the teachings of both of these anointed men of God. I told someone it was like that old song, "Trying to Love Two Ain't Easy to do…it started out as lots of fun but then I was torn.

Terry McNulty and I meet on the job and develop an instant relationship. I am immediately drawn to her. It was, and still is, one of the best relationships I've had. She introduced me to her cousin, Irene, who became Nikki and my hairdresser. They both suffer from some serious mental problems so I think it's hereditary.

Terry encourages me and I do the same for her. She listens when I rant about various things. She invited me to be a part of Sisters of the Word Book Club. Another set up for sure. I go to the first meeting and just love how the discussions flow regarding the book read. It is very interesting to hear others perspective on the same book. Join a book club. It will expand your thinking.

Deborah Banks is another one I'm drawn to like a magnet. She's a Christian and better yet, a believer. We have and continue to encourage each other. Deborah is involved in so many great activities in helping within the community. She doesn't talk it, she walks it. By the way, she's a "*PK*" (preacher's kid).

Slowly, the relationships with my biological family members start to be restored. Then friends or acquaintances I had been estranged from for years started to make contact. Isn't it amazing how when you're flat on your butt, down on your luck, and need these people, and they never call? At any rate, I am thankful to God for restoration.

After losing both apartments in one day we move back to my sister's for a few months. "God, I am so tired of living with other people. I appreciate the fact that I have a place to stay but I am tired."

Why did I tell Him this? Did He cause this? No, I did. Procrastination robs one of many blessings.

Nikki graduates in the top fifteen in her class at David Starr Jordan High School! Yes!!! Prior to graduation, the entire senior year, they go on so many trips...Six Flags, playing miniature golf, just too many trips. For the Junior Senior Prom she was absolutely lovely!

We had a champagne party using Sparkling Cider at Dorothy's. She had her own limousine, wore her tiara and just looked stunning. Robert's sister, Johnnie, came by as with a few others bearing gifts. (Johnnie and I met and another love connection was made) Many pictures were taken. Today is your day Nikki. You go girl!

God had given her such favor with the teachers, counselors and principal there. She was involved with not only band but choir and dance as well. The girl's musically inclined. She get it from her Momma.

She gets a California Grant to go to towards the furthering of her education from the school at graduation. God is awesome!

Dorothy and I travel to Louisiana in August of 2005. It was my first trip back there since I left. My primary reason is to go back and get my personal items that had been stored. Well, that's not true. The main reason was to go back for a celebration that we had planned for my aunt and several other family members; to get a chance to visit with and see family.

Sadly though, by the time the celebration took place we had lost two of the honorees...my aunt and my cousin. When we came together it was a time of rejoicing and a time of mourning. I was somewhat disappointed as I had hoped it would have been a big turn out. Letters had been sent out well in advance to people from all over but the turn out was not what I had hoped it would be. We still had a good time though.

My aunt has worked endlessly for any and every one all of

her life. If you think I complained about my running for others, mine paled in comparison to that she did. She's done this **all** of her life. How in the world could the people not come?

One of the reasons I believe, is because it was just before Katrina hit. Even though we were on the opposite end of the State and not directly affected by it, there was much rain in the area. Some people said when they started to come, there was a big downpour and they were unable to make it.

Dorothy and I went and stayed about a week. She had a ball visiting people she had not seen in years. Did I rest or even really get to visit anyone much while there? The answer is no. I got off the plane running. First it was to Wal-Mart, then on to DI's house to make some sausage balls and finally making it to get a few hours of sleep.

The next day it was off to the stores again, to the Forestry building to put up decorations, get the food together and all of that. Today was the day for the big event.

I, along with Kinete, Shie, Dee Dee, Della and DI, worked my butt off. Running this place and that one…tired, exhausted. I end up getting dressed at the Forestry Building for the event.

The overall thing went well. We had fun and that was what mattered. My aunt and a few others were pleased, and that pleased all of us.

The next day and the rest of my visit there I spend visiting some, checking with Robert to be sure he's going to drive my furniture and stuff to California for me, moving boxes, loading the truck, just running. By the time we get ready to leave I feel as if I need another vacation.

Okay, so I've already gotten furniture in California, what was so important about getting the furniture, clothing and other items here? Number 1, I felt like I was living in two places at the same time and it was driving me. I felt it was time to put closure to Minden and I thought by moving my stuff to California a closure would take place. That didn't happen until later.

I have tons of books on subjects covering practically everything. After Rev. Robert White came and brought my stuff to me, the Lord asked me one day if it was worth it. I felt as though getting my books alone was worth the trip. Reading is fundamental. I just love to read. My pictures and a few keepsakes from my grandmother, aunt and Pops who are all deceased were equally important. I am a sentimentalist and have to have some heritage around me.

We make the return trip to California. Guess what happened? We had purchased our original round trip tickets from a lady that one of Dorothy's friends knew. She claimed she worked at a travel agency, and we paid her roughly eight hundred dollars for two round trip tickets, got the tickets and went on our merry way. Well, Long Beach airport allowed us to travel using the tickets but not Shreveport. We were apprehended before boarding the flight by the Airport Police. What you say? You heard me right.

Dorothy is seventy two and she's sitting there bawling like a baby. Not me as I had my money order receipt for the ticket purchase and the person's phone number. They were not taking us to jail. We had done nothing wrong but stupidly bought tickets from someone trying to get a deal and they ended up being ***hot***!

The tickets had been purchased with a stolen credit card. The cardholders' last name just happened to have been "Mixon". They eyed me suspiciously, asked me for the credit card that had been used for the purchase and interrogated us. I'm being a bit dramatic now. Seriously though, they would not let us travel on our return flight even when we offered to pay. We were delayed for hours.

Finally, we were allowed to purchase tickets for an additional eight hundred and fifty dollars and return home. Dorothy vowed she'd never return there again. Why was she upset with them? They were only doing their job.

When we made it back to California, I contacted the person we purchased the tickets from. She gave some lame excuse and said she would give us a refund. To this day, we have not received one penny and really don't expect to. With the scams she's pulling, she's probably in jail by now.

Let me interject something here; don't assume I am normal now by any means. Just because this particular Chapter does not have a lot of "God said" and "God showed" doesn't mean it stopped. "Oh contraire!" I get back into in the last and final chapter of this book. Just be patient, I assure you more is coming. I just thought you might be interested in knowing this.

Back to work I go. This trip really messed me up. Instead of putting closure to the past, it seems I had more of a yearning and longing to go back. One day I asked my supervisor if he had heard the song, "Midnight Train to Georgia" and he said he had. Well, I say, LA has proved too much for me and I'm leaving. That repeated at different intervals from 2004 through mid 2006. I know he got sick of me.

I didn't immediately get back into church. Apparently I still had to go around a few more blocks. I hadn't let go of Minden. How could I really commit to a church or anything else as long as I was holding on? I couldn't and it was driving me and everyone around me.

Many starts were made but the minute things got a bit hard I was ready to run back to Minden. Commitment was not something I was ready to do fully with anyone. So, from August 2005 through December 2006, I was in and out of church. Trinity Broadcasting Network once more and again became my main means of staying spiritually motivated and educated. Thank God for Trinity Broadcasting Network!!!

In September 2005, Nikki and I find another apartment, this

time it was closer to my job. Before I was about thirty five to forty minutes away mainly due to heavy traffic and having to drop some things off at Nikki's school. Being closer to the job makes it so much easier for me when the bottom drops out later.

This apartment is small as was the other place we lived in. The major difference between this one and the previous one is the closets are larger and my bedroom is larger. At the old place we had more space in the dining room and our own laundry room. We also had a view of the street as opposed to looking out of the window at a brick wall.

The old place provided me with my own garage which served as storage and saved me money as I didn't have to purchase a separate storage space and we had a front and back yard. It was quiet there. I miss that place. You really sometimes don't know what you have until it's gone.

As of today, we are still in the apartment. After reflecting over all of the various changes we've gone through I immediately start to praise God for this place and the one before. Everything comes up short when I compare it to the house and land we had in Louisiana. There was plenty of closet space, two bathrooms, a laundry room, a huge family room, living room, formal dining room, large kitchen and plenty of parking spaces. Oh well, no sense in dwelling on what was. I am truly grateful for the things I have.

I actually like California. The only thing I don't like about it is the high cost for housing. It seems one pays a lot more to get so much less. Really, I should say Los Angeles. Traveling to other parts allowed me to see that there are many places in the state that are not as congested as Los Angeles and more affordable.

Christmas 2005 begins a turning point somewhat in my life. It is at that time I decide I am not going to mope and moan and complain about how much I miss people but instead enjoy it right where I am and I did. I've got my book club, my church (I attend sometimes), and some new friends. I'm grateful!

In early 2006, Annette Jones Davidson contacts me and a few other classmates. From these conversations, Women of Purpose and Determination came about. We started online book and Bible studies, online praise parties, online prayers and had many telephone calls. We studied "The Purpose Driven Life" and "Your Best Life Now" for the first year. Jackie Graham-Chapman sent us daily inspirational messages. Cynthia "Tan" Combs served as our PR person in Minden. Rose Thornton Jiles became a *big* mouthpiece for the group as with Marzetta Wright-Murray, Audrey Flournoy, Barbara Johnson-Smith, Jackie Lewis-Rice and Beverly Kennon.

We shared successes, encouraged each other, shared difficulties faced; we bonded. All of these women are from the Minden High School class of 1975. Some still reside in Minden and others live in different states. Barbara is actually in Japan.

Barbara took the lead in providing scriptures and reminders for our one day a week fast. We fasted and prayed on that day for so many people and so many things. These are anointed women.

Jeannette Bell, Gloria Morris, Janelle Thornton, Patricia Key and others came on board. Angela Wills, a great, anointed soloist, graced the group with her melodious voice at one of the meetings. The meetings were held once a quarter and initially were done at the Chamber of Commerce in Minden. I have not been able to attend any but that's about to change.

As of this time, the group is planning to celebrate its one year anniversary on March 17, 2007, at the Minden Community House. We've decided whether there are twenty five people, fifty or one hundred, we will have a grand time praising God. We know that everything that ever grew started out small. We definitely don't despise the days of small beginnings.

"Sisters of the Word Book Club" is going strong still. I haven't attended these events as I have desired to. That's about to change as well. Rosemary Couch is the person who takes this fully to heart and keeps everyone in line and motivated. She and Deborah Banks sort of each say it's the other. The one common thing is the love that both, no all, share for books and sharing.

Rae Jones, Betty "Scottye" Price, Terry McNulty, Treva Blackwell, Arlisa, Jamila, Vendetta, all are a part of this wonderful group and I believe more are coming.

This club has been in existence for several years. The list of books read is very impressive, very diverse, and are many. If you get nothing else from this book, please learn the value in reading.

I will not bore you with any more pertaining to all of this. Now, we move into the next chapter... **"God's Storehouse".**

CHAPTER SIX
God's Storehouse

"Ye are cursed with a curse: for ye have robbed me, even this whole nation. Bring ye all the tithes into the storehouse, that there may be meat in mine house and prove me now herewith, saith the Lord of hosts, if I will not open you the windows of heaven, and pour you out a blessing, that there shall not be room enough to receive it."

Malachi 3:9-10

There has been so much talk about **God's Storehouse** in previous chapters, along with speculations and comments as to what it is and what it is not. So what is actually **God's Storehouse**? What relevance does the above scripture have to supplying the answer to that question?

Malachi 3:9-10 states that we are cursed with a curse. Why are we cursed? Well, the scripture goes on to say that the curse came upon us because we robbed God in tithes and in offerings. What does this have to do with the questions asked above? Continue reading.

Some of you are probably thinking as you are reading this, I am and have always been a tither; have actually given more than my tithes and offerings as I support numerous ministries so why is there still a curse in reference to finances, relationships, health issues, etc. You think ... I give and give, yet nothing is happening. Let's delve into this a bit.

The tithe is a tenth of your gross earnings. In biblical days how did people tithe? Did they have money or did they give goods such as a portion of their crops or whatever goods they had received? I know I am asking plenty of questions but this is to get your juices flowing and your thinking caps on. Later in this chapter I will address all of this, so bear with me.

To remove the mystery now, ***God's Storehouse*** is simply stated each community, each family taking care of its own and as God provides the increase, enlarging our territory and bringing others into the family. ***God's Storehouse*** is about sharing information with others to remove the lack of knowledge as described in Hosea 4:6. ***God's Storehouse*** is about each man or woman that professes to be a man or woman of God teaching and attempting to reach others using biblical principles and encouraging him/her to become a part of His family. ***God's Storehouse*** is about each Christian adopting the philosophies..." Help Me To Help You", "Family Taking Care of Family", and "Together We *CAN* Make It Happen".

God's Storehouse is not just a lifelong ministry for me but should be for every person who serves as a representative for Christ. ***God's Storehouse*** is about doing everything in a spirit of excellence; building character; teaching our young women to be virtuous women and our young men to be the kings as God designed them to be. (Titus 2) He does have a divine order.

To answer the question brought up earlier; you're a tither, a giver so why does money seem to flow right out of your pockets? It seems there are holes and instead of it increasing it steadily goes down. Frustration seeps in. Believe this; God's divine plan is for us to put Him first in our finances. How are we to do this? Read the scripture above—tithes and offerings. Next we should take care of our own households. Now, taking care of our own households include not only meeting the regular household expenses but including in your budget (yes, I said the "B" word) money for miscellaneous expenses. Miscellaneous expenses include entertainment, auto repair, family vacations, things of that nature. If one fails to plan they plan to fail. We have to learn to be good stewards over our money as Christians. There are numerous books and tapes out there about money management His way. Buy the books. Listen to the tapes. Apply the knowledge.

God's Storehouse is about learning, growing, praying, playing, teaching, a place to partner, networking, being visionaries, removing limits off God, reading the word and other motivational/inspirational books, paving the way for others to dare to dream—it's about a revival of the Bible.

God's Storehouse is about recognizing that we are one body—HIS—and each member plays a vital role in the success of the rest of the members. It's recognizing that we do need each other to survive and to build up His kingdom. Is *God's Storehouse* a church? No, it's about getting in the churches that God has strategically placed each person in and helping that church to grow using your God given gifts, talents, knowledge, skills, connections and whatever God has given you to help to build up His church.

God's Storehouse is being under the leadership of anointed Pastors who preach to all about what we need to do and allow us to use our God-given skills to teach to others the "how-to" as far as carrying out the assignment. I've heard a preacher tells people what needs to be done and a teacher tells and shows one how to do it. Go where you're welcomed and accepted for who you are and where your gifts can be used. The Bible states that your gift will make room for you and bring you before great men. The Bible also says for us to not despise the days of small beginnings. So, if your church is small or large, you still have a part to play in its success. Know your place. "Obey them that have the rule over you, and submit yourselves: for they watch for your souls, as they that must give account that they may do it with joy, and not with grief: for that is unprofitable to you." Hebrews 13:17.

God's Storehouse is not duplicating or should not duplicate any activities but should rather meet the needs of those within the family and extend it to those outside the family in the general community that you happen to be a part of. Join an organization that has a passion that is one shared by you. Get involved. Become a supporter. God gives us similar visions, often times not for us to do solo acts, but to join forces with others already doing this to be more effective. There are many great causes out there.

Is your dream or vision to go into other hurting cities or countries and minister to those there by meeting needs? Maybe, just maybe, you cannot actually go or you have no real desire to go yet you want to help. Support a ministry spiritually and financially that's already doing this. In doing so, you are still helping to fulfill the great commission— Partnership.

God's Storehouse is not characterized by race, creed or color but rather by one common cause…kingdom building. It is not about any one religion but rather about all and lifting up the name of Jesus. God does not see any one particular group as being superior to another and neither should we. We are all family.

God's Storehouse is about removing ignorance, providing assistance, and removing that "I got mine, you get yours the best way you can" mentality. It is about changing a generation; changing a way of thinking. It is about breaking generational curses and starting generational blessings. In Isaiah, the scripture states to remember ye not the former things, nor the things of old, for behold I will do a new thing. God is ready to do a new thing in the lives of those who love Him.

God's Storehouse should begin in the homes of each Christian, extend to the church and as He enlarges our territory, out to the community, on our jobs and wherever we go. It's about being *bold* witnesses.

The Word of God states for us to not forsake the assembling

of ourselves as is the manner of some. (Hebrews 10:25) Does this just apply to assembling in church? No. As Christians, we should assemble together everywhere giving glory to God. You should see a sister or brother in a grocery store and get to praising God for whatever He's done. (Don't get so deep. They may just call the police on you as when the praises start it gets mighty hard to stop them. On the other hand, some unbeliever may come up to see what you're high on and get saved. One never knows.)

    God's Storehouse is a life-style change. It's about no longer believing the lies of the enemy but rather the word of God. **God's Storehouse** is living a purpose driven life, recognizing that each of us as Christians have one common purpose, "*Go ye therefore, and teach all nations, baptizing them in the name of the Father, and of the Son, and of the Holy Ghost; teaching them to observe all things whatsoever I have commanded you; and lo, I am with you always, even unto the end of the world*". Amen! *Matthew 28:19-20*

    So, if **God's Storehouse** is all of this where do I give my tithes and offerings? Well, my understanding, and please realize that I say "my" understanding is that the tithes and offerings should go to support your local body. (There are many great Bible scholars out there who I'm sure will gladly let me know if I'm wrong. I welcome the feedback.) However, I am a firm believer that one should give the way God leads and instructs him to give. What do you mean by that Prophetess?

    When you have a relationship with God and He is ordering and directing your steps, He may lead you to give to some and it makes no sense at the time. He may actually have you to sow into many ministries as He has done with me over the years. My only response is to be obedient to the Holy Spirit as far as His leading and directing you as to where you sow your seeds. Read Luke 8 starting with verse 5. This gives the parable of the sower. So, again I say, be obedient always to the Holy Spirit regardless of what anyone says or thinks. It's a fact that understanding does come later.

Back to more about ***God's Storehouse,*** why is there a whole chapter dealing with this in this particular book? Isn't this something that most people deal with already? We know this so why are you telling us something that we already know? Simply put, the Bible tells us to not be hearers of the word but doers also. In hearing and not doing, the word says we deceive ourselves. Yes, that's right... <u>we deceive ourselves!</u> Many times we blame the enemy for deceiving us when actually its self-deception because we hear a word, read a word and then think because we know a word we're okay. That is self-deception.

I'll give you an illustration. If you were to bake a cake, you would first get your recipe out and then follow the instructions. But, just suppose for a minute, you decided to bake a cake having never baked one before, and you say I'll do it without the recipe. Well, number one, I wouldn't want any of that cake as you've deceived yourself into thinking that you are going to bake the perfect cake minus the recipe. If by chance you were to know the ingredients, but not the exact measurements, that cake would be a mess.

If you omitted any of the ingredients or the proper measurements, chances are the cake would be a total flop and you'd be disappointed. But why? You chose to do it without the instructions. Well, it's the same way in life, if we want to know how to live and do it God's way but never choose to read and follow the instructions, then we definitely deceive ourselves... be doers. (In II Timothy 2:15, the Bible tells us to study. Don't allow others to do all of the work for you—study)

I'll take it a step further. Suppose you dream of becoming a homeowner, business owner, doctor, lawyer, Indian chief. Yet, you never invest the time in doing the necessary studying, acquire proper certification and research to make it happen and God forbid you should learn the information and not apply it... deceiving yourself.

Okay, so I veered of the path for a slight second. But when you think about it, not really because all of this is what **God's Storehouse** is about. Being a visionary...how many of you had visions, dreams, goals and some well-meaning person told you for whatever reason you could not achieve or attain them. Read your Bible. The word says "I can do all things through Christ who gives me strength."

How many times have you heard, "You got pregnant and ruined your life" or "Dropping out of high school ruined your chances of doing anything with your life" or better yet, "Nothing good is ever going to come of you because you got bad blood". The devil is a liar. Read your Bible. The word says greater is He that is in you than he that is in the world.

Don't be deceived either by Satan or yourself. Don't allow others to tell you what you can or cannot do. There are people who are physically and/or mentally handicapped and living successfully. There are some that other people counted out that have succeeded against all odds. There are many people out there who refuse to believe the lies of the enemy because they know Who and Whose they are. They not only know this, but they read the book that has been laid out before them and continue to go against the grain, so to speak. Never allow someone else to define who you are.

Read the biographies of people you consider to be successful. Read of their struggles, isolation, ups and downs. They all paid the price for their success.

It is not over in anyone's life until God says it's over. It is not wise to count anyone out. The wiser thing to do is to help that brother or sister with a hand up...that is if that person wants it. We always have choices.

"Know your limits and when you've reached yours know that God is able to do exceeding, abundantly

above all that we ask or think according to the power that works in us". Ephesians 3:20.

Pray because prayer does change things. Write in a journal your daily experiences. Read, apply, believe and take a stand. We've all heard that saying if you don't stand for something you'll fall for anything.

Wake Up. Get Up. Stay Up. Pray Up. Rise Up. Praise Up. Look Up. I love that old song, "No Matter How High I Get, I'll Still Be Looking Up to You". No matter how high God takes us in life we will always have "Look Up".

Stay focused on your mission; faithful to your cause and you will end up being fruitful and hear God say, "Well done thy good and faithful servant, you've been faithful over few things, I'll now make you ruler over much."

God's Storehouse is about providing temporary housing to those who find themselves displaced due to reasons beyond their control or to newlyweds as a means of helping them to acquire the funds and knowledge needed to branch out on their own. Let me just add that by teaching them before hand what a Godly man and woman should be, they should know and wait. Remove the excuses. God has a divine order and it's written where—in His word. The truth is though, most don't wait. So what do we do? Do we just continually say, "I told you not to marry him or her.", "I told you to wait." or do we try to reach them and assist them in getting it together. We do the latter only if they're willing and obedient. Otherwise, let them go. If one does not do it early on, I guarantee there will be much pain later. People have to go through what they have to go through. Know your limits.

God's Storehouse is about helping young people that are starting out by teaching them God's way as to what marriage is all about. No where in the word does it say He approves of shacking. So, we should not encourage or tolerate it either. If they choose to follow their own way, well read Hebrews 10:26. We must be willing to give the people the truth. That's what sets one free.

It is about assisting them as well as others that you know of in need with furniture, dishes and the likes to get a new start or a fresh start after a disaster. It is about connecting people with resources that can help eliminate needs in their lives and it is definitely about sharing with others the word of God. The first shall be last and the last shall be first.

God's Storehouse is about business start-ups. By doing your homework, networking with others and launching out. It opens the door for not only the business owner to be blessed but the ability to bless others through your services you provide and by providing jobs to those seeking employment. He gives the same promise to us as He did Abraham in Genesis. It's in the word.

God's Storehouse is about realizing dreams. Success has many definitions. One person's definition of success or "arriving" may be in getting a high school diploma. Another's may be becoming a homeowner. Yet others may dream of obtaining a degree. The list is endless and exhausting. The point I would like to make here is life is a journey and as we move from glory to glory, after attaining one level we should continue to stretch. Don't become complacent—stretch, grow, and get out of your comfort zones. It's about doing yourself first and encouraging others to follow. Build it. They will come.

God's Storehouse is about so many things. The first word says it all—it's about God first. It's about faith. It's about love. It's about trust. It's about hope. It's about knowing you may fall many times but get back up, brush yourself off and start over again. It's about doing unto others as you would have done unto you. It's all about believing the Word of God. The same promises God gave in biblical times, He gives to us today. Believe and receive them. The Word is real!

Hopefully you know now what ***God's Storehouse*** is and hopefully you, too, will come on board and be a part of this great family. Who is ***God's Storehouse***? All of us and we need you to survive.

We've all missed the mark. We've all made the mistakes. We've all had our falling outs now let's put all of that behind us and press towards the mark. Let's really walk the walk that we just love to talk. Satan's plan—divide and conquer. God's plan—unite and win and we will. I have faith.

Lastly, keep it real. Be you—the authentic person He designed you to be. Don't be so heavenly minded you're no earthly good and I say welcome to the family.

> *And Jabez called on the God of Israel, saying, Oh that thou wouldest bless me indeed, and enlarge my coast and that thine hand might be with me, and that thou wouldest keep me from evil, that it may not grieve me. And God granted him that which he requested."*
>
> *I Chronicles 4:10*

It feels so good to be free
And free to no longer plead
By being free, and free indeed
God has removed needs
Now, let me see—what did I really lose?

I lost a <u>lot</u> of money
And material things
I lost TV's, VCR's, and gold chains
Diamonds and rings

I pawned and lost stereo's, CD's & videos
I even pawned and lost
My daughter's Nintendo

There were Nintendo tapes
Amplifiers, the list goes on and on

I put thousands of miles on my old car
Running here, there and yonder
Never running away from God
But rather to and for Him
In pursuing this ministry

I left a job making big bucks
Because God said to pursue this ministry
I told folk from the very beginning
It was *never* about me.
There's been humiliation, shame and rejection
My children have gone without much
These are the things given up
But believe you me, we gained **MUCH**

This ministry from its very inception
Was one of a "coming together?"
Sharing information, lifting up Jesus
So that lack would be removed forever
I wouldn't take anything for my journey

Because God finally set me free
And, for those who know your Bible
You know, He who the Son sets free is free indeed

Now, I've been broke, busted and disgusted
But from this day forward I won't be anymore
I am going to people who I **know** can be trusted
And now knocking on the right doors

This ministry is in my heart
God knows beyond a shadow of doubt
That I have done my part

Now to those that rejected God's plan
I really pray blessings over you
Because you can say no to me
But in the end, "Who is mere man
To reject His ministry?"

I won't beg, plead or ask anymore
You see, I don't have to
God whipped me in line with His will for my life
And He'll do the same for each of you

I love still and forgive all
If you should decide you need me
Just give me a call

Other things we went without
Were lights, gas, cable and telephone
By Wednesday of this week
They will all be on

I pawned and lost many things
To send countless letters and obtain information for you
If you don't need or want my help
Then God bless you

We may not be on this Street
Maybe in close range
Chances are the address
And the phone numbers will change

I've said to many "help me to help you"
And by doing so, you'll only help yourself
After today I won't ask anymore
And I'll no longer offer any help

One should not have to plead with folks
To get them to do God's will
I have continually tried to though
And God keeps telling me to just "be still"

It's so hard for me to just be still
When there is so much lack
God tells me to be quiet now
Because He has got my back

People, you know I've bugged you and bugged you
To the point that many call me a pest
And, in order for me to not send you any more "last letters"
Come together and let's pass the test

What is the test? Do you really want to know?

Well, this much I will tell you
The real test I believe, the one God wants us to pass
Is who **really** believes His word is true?

If you, like me, believe and know it is
Then my question to you is this
Why have we not come together?
So we can get on with this?

God set me free to plead no more
He set me free from a lot of things
But if you will now open a door
The next voice will be mine you hear
At the end of the telephone ring

Where do you stand? Who's on the Lord's side?
If we're truly there
Why do we run and hide?

I know all are very busy
Doing worthwhile things for the Lord
But do you believe by coming together
The tasks may not be so hard

I'm tired right now and I need some rest
As God now will show all
I am one of His best

Forsaking All I Trust HIM!!! **FAITH**	

Together	**T**otal
Everyone	**E**ffort of
Achieves	**A**ll
More if there is	**M**embers

CHAPTER SEVEN
And Then There Was Glory

As we enter into the final Chapter of this book, I will continue with a bit more of some daily events and discussions taking place between God and me, me and others, and of course, the enemy and I. Before going into this, please allow me to recap for a minute.

God said Robert would do certain things and as I've already stated, I met several Robert's along the way. When it all first began I only knew one Robert and pestered him much. Hearing "Robert" all the time, I tried to <u>make</u> this one person do all of the things God said Robert would do. There were so many other things that He said Robert would do, too many to include in this writings. Needless to say, I drove that one crazy.

Robert Taylor , Robert Lee , Robert Mason , Robert Branch, Robert Tilton, Robert Watford , Rev. Robert White , Robert Holeman , Robert Nubine, Robert at FEW Federal Credit Union, and Robert Kiyosoki . Each and every one of these Robert's helped and did what God said they would do. There will probably be more to come.

Did I seek out Robert's only? No, it seemed that anytime I asked someone to refer me to someone to get anything done, it would be a Robert. Why? Because God said Robert would do all of these things and they had to be because God does not lie.

Have all of the manifestations taken place in my life that God said would happen? No. Then why am I finishing this book now when the story is not over? I do it simply because it is time. This will hopefully peak your curiosity to read the next book to see how it all ends and if I am who I say and God says I am. There is so much that I could not write in this book, things that God said but I assure you the next one will be all inclusive. For anyone who wants to read the original handwritten and typed worn daily pages done, I welcome it, maybe?

Well, I said you would read of my three different weddings at the beginning of this book and you will. Actually, in this writing I've had more than three. I was married to my first husband. My second husband and I married twice and I married the Lord. But two more marriages took place here. Are you confused or have you figured it out?

What is a marriage? It's a partnership. I've heard it said it is two or more partners in the same ship traveling together in the same direction. It's a mutually committed relationship. So, have you figured it out yet?

Let me answer this for you. My next marriage, so to speak, occurred when I became committed to my job with the Social Security Administration. Does that sound strange to you? Think partnership. Before I answer the question to the last marriage covered in this book, allow me to finish this story.

Now, in recapping a bit more, please remember at one point in the book God did say that different people would do certain things than those I originally believed would. Did I get my wires crossed in the messages I received from Him? If God does not lie then why are different people doing them than those originally given? Everything boils down to choices.

God presents each of us with choices daily. He has a definite plan for each of our lives. He does not force His will on any. There are many people in the cemetery with dreams and visions that never manifested for one reason or another. No one is irreplaceable and I mean no one. God presents us with people and opportunities. Some will be obedient and others won't. It is biblically sound.

Will God allow anyone to hold up His program? No, He will just use those that are willing and obedient. You've heard that saying, "One monkey don't stop no show"? Well, it's true. One of my many problems was looking back so much, longing for those originally given me to come on board and go the distance with me and ignoring the ones who were saying "let's go".

It was only later that I realized that in life it is like a relay race so to speak. In this type of race a runner goes so far and then passes the baton on to others and it continues until the race is over. That's how it is in life.

I've heard it said that many times you want certain people to go the distance with you but they can't. God allows us to go so far and then passes the baton to someone else. We have to realize and recognize when the change has taken place and be flexible enough to adapt to the new environment, embracing and accepting the new runners in the race. We may want to go the distance with people but each of us has our race to run, some together and some individually.

Growth takes place when we recognize the chosen path God has for us and pursue it with passion. Maturity takes place when we get to the point to where we fully accept ourselves and the path lay out before us regardless of what anyone says or thinks. Spiritual maturity takes place when we can recognize the voice of the Holy Spirit, study the word and adhere to the leadings.

The next few pages will cover the period from July 2, 2006 through January 7, 2007. It will be written a bit differently than chapter four. I'll just basically cover the things I think

important. This was covered before but bears repeating now, the entire objective of this book is to encourage the reader to do whatever one *believes* God has placed in them, say whatever one *believes* He leads you to say and be whatever you *believe* He wants you to be. It is to let you know that one plus God is a majority and any dream is attainable if you just believe, step out, persevere and complete. The writing of this book is my giving birth and proof that dreams do come true. It's taking care of God's business.

Sunday, July 2, 2006

I wake up writing a love letter to God. In this letter I tell Him of my love for Him and I just say thank you. Thanking Him for everything that He has done is my goal and my hearts desire this day.

In this letter, I do tell Him (He already knows) about the identity theft issue that's taken place in my life. I thank Him for the blessing (this time) in being financially challenged. If I had money in the account the thieves tried so many times to get into, I would have been really robbed. As it was, there was very little money there and the checks presented for payment could not be cashed. I thanked Him for my detecting this early. I thanked Him for being God.

There is a situation that I bring before Him, one that deals with my house being out of order. I allowed a young man to come here and stay. It was to have been just for a couple of weeks. After saying yes I began to be convicted. I asked Him for guidance.

This young man was displaced due to circumstances beyond his control. At the time that I said yes I did not get the full story. I honestly thought I was doing something good. He was in school, trying to better his life and ended up losing his housing. How could my allowing him to stay here not be a good thing?

Let me tell you how. Number one, this young man and my daughter were dating. Did I open the door wide for Satan to come in? Yes, I did **but** I thought it would only be for a couple of weeks **and** told the both of them that I wanted no *"hanky panky"* of any sort taking place here. Naïve. What young person wouldn't take advantage of a situation like that? (Older ones would too)

The one thing I do not believe in is shacking. My first husband and I lived together a few months before we got married. Going to church, hearing the word and being convicted because of shacking caused me to jump into a marriage that never should have taken place. Shacking is in no way God's will. Yet, I opened the door and Satan walked in. I did the same thing to them that had been done to me.

Let me contradict myself here. Yes, I am doing that. The first marriage should have taken place because out of it came my daughter. Children are a gift from God. The best thing from the marriage was her. Since our lives are already predestined before we were even thought about, it should have happened.

Back to this shacking thing, talk about my whippings I got while he was here, I could not rest. Going to bed at night, tossing and turning and wrestling became a nightly thing for me. I'm compromising my beliefs. Compromising only causes one to lose. Knowing this, why do I allow it to continue for about three days short of seven months? Read on. Remember, we are tested and tried to perfect us. Life is a continual series of classes. We pass some and fail even more.

Did I really fail this one? I am going to let you decide for yourself. Keep in mind that for me "God's Storehouse" is a lifetime ministry and provides temporary housing for those displaced due to reasons beyond their control. Bear in mind it is about encouraging and teaching, especially our young. Now, did I fail this test? No.

Have you lost your mind Regina? The mistake I made was in not getting an understanding of all of the facts beforehand. The mistake I made was not going to God before saying yes. The mistake I made was in trying to handle this situation alone. It does take a whole village to train our young.

Help was offered but after a while I begin to think this is my house and having everyone put their two cents in means I can't control my own house so I politely declined some help offered. Now you know I needed the help as I had a young man in my household and no husband as the head to help steer me and guide me. We women can be emotional and often act or react out of emotions instead of using plain old common sense. That goes out the door many times. It's the way we, or some of us, are.

I will go on to say that this young man helped me much to

recognize some areas in which I needed to improve. Not only that, he became a member of "The Word of God" (Church), sang in the choir, and he and Nikki both danced with "Here2Prayze". Just as a side note, Here2Prayze is an awesome praise dance ministry. Under the leadership of Britani Dixon, they have traveled many places and will go even further. Many of you will get the privilege of seeing for yourself.

On this particular day, I pour my heart out to God. He said to me, "Regina, I now know I can trust you. You have stood in spite of the attacks (sound familiar?) of the enemy and continually praised me. You have passed the test and now I will send you everything you need. I put you in a position to help many and you will."

He tells me that He has opened doors for Nikki with a job with the Social Security Administration. He goes on to say the easiest thing in the world to do is run. Sometimes the hardest thing in the world to do is to stay where you are.

He proceeds to tell me that this young man was not put in our lives by accident and that he will help me much and I him. (We did and will continue to.) He goes on to tell me that people need to know that it is all about Him; it is all about kingdom building. He tells me a lot but these things are for me only.

Then He tells me to go back to church, get back into my exercise routine, study the word, read inspirational books, listen to the word, go to my book club meetings and get out and have some fun. He says that He is not a God that wants people miserable but rather one that wants people to prosper in every area of their lives.

He says that He will never bless me just for me and now He is reversing the curse and setting me free to be the real me. He tells me again to quit smoking. No, I haven't stopped, at least not yet.

I write many other prayers—thanking Him for The Word of God, Pastor Snead and his family, Women of Purpose and Determination, Sisters of the Word Book Club, SSA, Here2Prayze,

Trinity Broadcasting Network, Creflo, City of Refuge, Nikki, Kendrick, Keisha, Kimmie, Khrystal, and all of my family members, for life, health and strength and for everything. I pray this prayer daily from July until the present date and my list of things and people to be thankful for continually grows. I pray God's blessings over them all and on the days that our group fasts and prays, I ask God to bless each of those listed above in a special way.

July 16, 2006

I type this. It was actually written about three weeks ago.

Somewhere along the way
I got lost in the hustle and bustle of life
So engrossed in what other's thought,
Others beliefs, others opinions
Until I lost me

Who I am
What my beliefs are
What my values are
What matters most

Trying to please everyone

But never truly pleasing me
Caught up in a web of confusion

Who am I?
What are my values?
What are my beliefs?

Living the way I believe
Really sets me free

It sets me free to love God
It sets me free to love and be me
It sets me free to love my family
Wherever they may be

Others have, what all of us have
Their opinions and their beliefs
I cannot allow theirs to determine and define
Who is the "real" me

I'll listen, take advice
And weigh it as it should be
But I will not, not another day
Allow others to define me

And that, my friend is the
Definition of being free….She found herself

It didn't happen until later.

    How and when did it happen? Well, in the beginning God told me that August was my month and it was. That was the month that I hit rock bottom. How did that happen? Thanks for asking but before I address that please allow me to say that over the years at various times, one by one God had me to drop weight in the form of holding on to people. Biological family members were the first and the hardest to let go of. It didn't happen all at once, it was a process.
    Then, I began to let go of other family members and many times I found myself standing alone. It was as it should have been.

The hardest ones to let go of in the sense of caretaking and meddling were my children. Nikki, my baby, was really hard but I passed the test. Just like when God told Abraham to offer up Isaac as a sacrifice but then He had a ram in the bush.

The tests were not for others. At least I don't think they were. The tests were to see if I would stand, if I truly believed that God loves people more than I, and that He knows what's best for all of us. The tests were so that God could see if He could trust me to say and do whatever regardless of what others said or think. I had to get to the point to where I put no one before Him. The tests were for me.

Now, to answer the question as to how rock bottom happened, purchasing a car in October 2005, I did all of the wrong things when I got it. I had a former car salesman take me to a car dealership in Louisiana and explained how to negotiate a deal when buying a new car. The problem with that was I felt that because my credit was still messed up I had no negotiating power and actually settled for a car I really didn't want in the beginning. I drove away in the car knowing I had paid too much for it and that I honestly could not afford the payments.

After the identity theft took place and so many other negative things not covered here, I got two payments behind on the car. The same day that I closed my bank account, filed a police report, contacted the Federal Trade Commission and the Credit Reporting Agencies was the day they came and picked up the car. I explained and even showed them the papers where I had been running around trying to get it resolved but I waited too late and was actually showing the papers to the wrong people.

That very day I immediately paid the two car payments but they had added a bunch of other charges. (Procrastination is a thief.) An application had been filed with another lender to lower the interest rate thereby lowering the actual payment amount to a price I could afford. I was told that after doing some things, which I did do, the application would be approved. I followed all the steps. And I waited, and waited, and waited.

Now during this period of waiting I did make regular phone calls to ensure that all was well. Many went unreturned and after the vehicle was repossessed I was told by the loan officer that they had actually denied my application and the person just didn't have the heart to tell me or send me a denial letter. What one does not know can cost a lot.

Afterwards, someone near and dear asked me how in the world could I lose a car making the kind of money I earn? I was asked if I had a gambling problem or a drug problem. I had neither. I had an addiction, one of trying to take care of everybody.

When one person would get in dire straits, I would rush in like mighty mouse because I just couldn't stand to see that person hurt. You know how he'd say, "Here I come to save the day?" Hurting myself and hindering the others growth many times is what I still continued to do.

Can you imagine how small I felt? I don't think so. It wasn't so much what the person said, but the fact that it was the truth and it did eventually set me free. I know this person cared about me because this person told me the truth with love in their heart. A real friend is never critical or judgmental. This person has done any and everything to help me and mine. Again, that's a friend.

Honestly, there had been others to tell me some things that I chose to ignore but God used this one to let me really see that it is insane to keep doing things the same way and expect different results. That's insanity!!!

Others have told me for about twenty years or more that I try to take care of too many people. My grandmother, Pops, my brother, my sister, and the list go on and on. The thing is, I had been doing what I had been taught and it was hard to break that habit.

God told me years ago, or rather asked me, "How dare you

say I don't supply your need? I give you more than enough. You keep going around putting out fires and hindering the works I am doing in others lives." Well, if even God said it, why did it take me so long to realize that what others said was true? All I can say to that is it was all a part of the plan and God knows who to use to get us to fully understand. Or maybe it was because I did it my way...just plain stubborn and hardheaded.

I'll just say thanks to that person because that actually was the beginning of a wake-up period. Sunday, August 6, I declared as my Emancipation Proclamation Day. It was another freedom day. He takes us from glory to glory. I declared, "Woman thou art loosed".

Can you imagine waking up from a long nightmare realizing that most of the things you have been taught in the past or rather told by well meaning people were not the truth? Can you imagine being told and shown constantly how to give to others and never being taught how to take care of yourself in a Godly, balanced way? Can you imagine the disappointment when you finally wake up to realize that you have spent forty nine years of lies, deceived by the enemy? Can you even begin to feel the pain?

The breakings had to occur. Can you imagine a person being so needy that they literally beg people to help them over and over again when God has given that person the power all along to help themselves?

Can you even begin to feel the humiliation and shame that one goes through in begging men and women to step up to the plate and be the men and women God created us to be, yet that person is not doing it themselves? What in the world have I been other than deceived?

I have seen some of the women in my family flash before my eyes, the huge sacrifices made, and now in their older years, still going through. Did not God say to obey is better than to sacrifice? Aren't our latter years supposed to be greater than our former years?

I know I am asking a lot of questions but I really want to get you to thinking. Are we supposed to help people? Most definitely. But we are to do it God's way.

Looking at my ex-husbands and other males I know that are not at all responsible caused me to let go of my son. If this is a glimpse of his future then I must let go and let God. I don't want him to be like that and neither does God.

The thought of my daughter growing up with this unnatural/ungodly false sense of responsibility causes me to do a lot of personal inventory and to make many changes. It is called walking the walk according to the word. It's time to change a generation!

I do know what we make happen for others, God makes happen for us. My only point in all of this is I will not ***think*** it's God leading, guiding and directing me, I will now really seek His wisdom and ***know*** that it is Him. Otherwise, it costs too much and it's not a price we have to pay. Jesus paid it all.

My daughter, as with every other young lady, needs to recognize her worth. Any man worth having will not ask you to compromise your beliefs. Any man worth having will work on getting himself together and allow you to do the same—God's way. Any woman who recognizes her worth will not take care of a man or allow one to bring her down. A real man would want to help build her up and not be a leech or a burden on her. A real man knows a woman's worth and recognizes God's gift to him in giving him that virtuous woman. ***A man who finds a wife, a Godly one, does find a good thing.***

I am no longer a caretaker. I am an anointed, blessed vessel to be used by God for His service. I am a woman first, a Godly woman second. I have needs in my life that only God can supply. The need for real love is the greatest and with God's unconditional love and my love and acceptance of me, the rest will follow.

My Pastor, Pastor Snead and his family have helped to restore my belief somewhat in my fellow man. Gail King also has done the same. They are true examples and are all anointed vessels of God. They are down to earth.

These people do not profess to be perfect. They walk the walk as God leads them. Please don't think that I in any way elevate them, I simply thank God for them as they are who they are—nothing more and nothing less.

They are good people, real people. It is their acts of kindness and love shown to me and mine that draws me back to The Word of God. It is the love shown to me and mine during this breaking period, the encouragement that thrusts me back into the ministry full force to do whatever I can, in whatever way I can to help to build up that church. It is their embracing us just as we are.

There are many good people in that church. It feels like home. It is home. Please allow me to add that I have met good people in each and every church I've been a part of.

Bottom line, it is their love, warmth, sincerity. That's what causes me to walk through the doors with determination and real commitment. I pray that God allows me and mine to be built up no place other than The Word of God Missionary Baptist Church for as long as we are in Los Angeles which I hope and pray will be for many years to come. I will just be a little different as I have to be the real me.

Okay, you keep harping on the real you. Who is the real Regina? The real Regina would not even think about not exercising. Having exercised pretty much for many years and then moving to California and just stopping—well that's not me. The real Regina is not as wimpy as this one over the past few years has been. The real Regina believes, I mean really believes in God and herself and does not accept defeat as an option. The real Regina loves to look good, loves a neat house and likes to have fun.

The real Regina (Yes Annette, it's true) enjoys having monthly dinners and music, games and fellowship. The real Regina is a tongue talking, praising woman of God. The real Regina loves talking and meeting new people. The real Regina likes some sports, boxing, playing dominos, dancing, singing, learning, reading, writing and growing.

The real Regina *is not* as bossy or meddlesome as this one has been. That's the real Regina and that's who I am going to be. I just got to be me.

Oh yeah, the real Regina knows how to manage her money (now), her time (now) her talents (now) and her house (now). That's me. Well, that's who I actually am when? One word—later. How much later? All we've heard is later, later when? By the time the book is published, that's when.

I'm still praying asking God to deliver me completely from cigarettes. Years ago Prophetess Helen Godfrey told me that God told her to tell me that He had supernaturally delivered me from the cigarettes before and I went back. She said He told her to tell me the next time would not be as easy. It has not.

I tried pills, patches and even attended a smoking cessation program. None of that worked. I've tried fasting and prayer and that has not worked. A couple of years ago I stopped smoking in the house and car thinking that last step would be easy. Again, it hasn't.

Sunday, August 27, 2006

Hello Lord,

It's me again. God, I want to thank you for the wonderful service we had today at The Word of God. The message was just for me!!! (And the rest of the congregation) What was the message? It was "Finding Your Purpose through Your Pain". The scripture reference was Genesis 41:51-52. Pastor Snead also incorporated into this message Mary and Martha's story from John 11.

What is so amazing is that Women of Purpose and Determination has been reading, studying and discussing "The Purpose Driven Life" now for a while. One of the Chapters recently covered deals with the very same subject. Are you trying to tell me something?

Pastor told the story of Joseph, from dream to reality; from the pit to the palace and the favor of God all the way. He talked about not sharing your vision with everyone *INCLUDING* those in the church. I know that's right because as he stated there are even haters in the church. I found that out the hard way.

Today I learned that Manasseh means to forget. Joseph had to forget all of the bad things that had happened to him in order for the promises to come to pass and so do we.

I pray for unity tonight— unity within our church, unity within Women of Purpose and Determination, unity on the job, unity with Sisters of the Word, unity in our homes, unity everywhere. We need it. United we stand and divided we fall.

Show me the way to go oh Lord. Teach me Your ways. This is my prayer. In Jesus name. Amen

Sunday, September 10, 2006 8:12 AM

Good morning God,

Have I told You lately how much I love you? Well, if not, I just want to say that I do love you so much. Thank You for all you have done for me and mine. Thank you for life, health, strength, a roof over my head, clothes on my back, shoes on my feet, many modes of transportation, a good family, my children's salvation and their working in the ministry. I could go on and on but suffice it to say, thank You for everything.

God, I ask that You forgive me of all my sins. I repent of anything that I have done or said that is not like You and ask Your forgiveness. Father, help me to be a better mother, friend, worker, student, employee, aunt, niece, singer, speaker, and yes, even a wife when the time comes. Help me to walk in Your ways and according to Your will.

Thank You Father for giving me the desires to get my life in order FIRST for Your glory, and to share with other women, young and old, of Your goodness. I pray for each and every one of my family members and God I have many scattered all over the world. I pray for each and every member of The Word of God Church and any other church or ministry I have been connected with in any way. I pray for the leaders of these great churches/ministries.

I pray for each and every member of Women of Purpose and Determination; for each and every one of my co-workers; for the men and women fighting a war for our freedom and for our leaders throughout the world.

I pray your blessings over each and every one of those mentioned above and ask that You supply, as only You can, each and every need in their lives. This is my prayer to you today.

I also pray for our communities, the saved and the unsaved. I ask You God to help people to realize that the killings and bickering are senseless and not like you. Help us all to realize that we can do more together than any of us can do apart. Help us God as we all stand in need of help in one way or another.

Help us all to keep first things first and stay focused on You. Help us all to share our testimonies and struggles with others. There is not one day, second, minute or hour that goes by that we don't need Your help.

Thank You, Lord, for total deliverance from cigarettes, getting my finances in order, the weight loss, both physical and emotional and for promotion. Thank You for helping me better plan my time each day so that I can accomplish all that You desire me to. I know Your word says to whom much is given, much is required. Lead me;

guide me, day by day. Order my steps in Your word. Help me to be a light that shines brightly for You.

I pray a special prayer for a dear friend today and ask that You mend that person's broken heart. I ask that You give that person a real purpose for living and lead that person into my family or rather Your family. God, I welcome all family members, those I know and those I don't know. I ask that You remove the pain and help that person get on fire for You.

I could go on and on but I'll end this now with praising You for all you've already done. This is the day that You have made. I will rejoice and be glad in it.

Your daughter,

Regina

God's reply—

Regina, I know you love Me. I know you love me so much. I am taking you to levels beyond your wildest dreams. You will stop smoking of that you can know and have no doubt. I have too much work in my plans for you.

I told you to form an alliance with you Pastor, Gail and Deacon King, Minister Smith and his wife, Kathy and some others there in your church. You are right, all of you will hit multi-millionaire status and it is for my glory. With them, you will walk the walk. I have a million and one ways to bless people. Watch My power!

I will lead, guide and direct you to fit in exercise, family time, financial training, computer training and many other things including fun things. I am working with you on a balanced life so that you can teach others. You will learn how to do this and walk the walk.

You can take the Real Estate Exam or you can do Mary Kay

or you can do both. The choice is yours. Either direction you choose, I will bless you.

Don't pressure yourself into thinking there is only one way. I have many ways to bless people. Regina, I love you. I love you all and by the seven of you coming together; working together to help build up the people and build up the church people will SEE my glory.

There will be some haters but don't even worry about them. Love the people. Love them My way. You don't even fully realize just how blessed you are. You are in for some shocks in your life and they will *all* be good ones.

I love you Regina. I am now going to show you and the world just how much I love you. Enjoy your day. Let me hear you say I am blessed. And, you are."

The next day God tells me He is not going to build me up as long as my house was out of order. What He was specifically referring to was the fact that I still was allowing this young man to live in my house when I did not need to. He says to me that play time has ended and this is not a game.

He said that this young man did help to open my blind eyes to even more things. He assured me that he is not a bad person, just young and in need of much teaching. He says it is time for him to go home.

He tells me that He is working on me on having a balanced life and there is no way I can teach others about balance when I am not doing it myself. Practice what you preach. He goes on to tell me that there is no way I can teach others about being a Godly woman, doing it His way when He has told and shown me His way through the written and spoken word and I am not practicing it. Walk the walk, He says.

He says, "Nikki needs rest. Nikki needs to schedule a physical. Nikki needs to get her bills in order. Nikki needs to go to the dentist.

Nikki needs to keep her job. Nikki needs to get a new car. Nikki has many needs and you, as a mother, are not being a good steward over the daughter that I gave you by allowing her needs to go unmet. Nikki is the most valuable asset I have given you. You do not have to or need to sacrifice her. That's out of My will.

Regina, I have told you for over a year or so that a certain person's role in your life ended a long time ago. You keep trying to think or believe that person to be the one. I told you that this person ***WAS*** my best for you, but because of his disobedience, he has now been replaced. I gave you the promise of a husband and that is what I am giving you. He will be one that recognizes you as an asset and recognizes and appreciates your worth

Get ready, Regina. I've told you all throughout to not be so sure about people. I told you changes were coming and they are. You are going to be oh so surprised when you come face to face with the person I have for you. This person is already a man of great means, a man after my own heart and one who will love you like no other. Wait for him. You have had your one night with the king. Get ready for a lifetime with the King.

Get yourself together now all the way. Do not make any more pledges. Pay those that you have made including your monthly partnerships and don't make any more until ALL of your debts are paid in full.

Regina, it is time for you to let go of each and every one of your immediate family members. You must let go in order for them to grow. This includes Nikki and Kendrick. Send Kendrick his box. (I did) Love them, but do not enable them anymore. You are actually doing more harm than good by giving them money and allowing them to be dependent on you. You are not allowing them to grow up. You are hindering their progress. Let go all the way now. I've got them and I will whip them in line with My will for their lives just as I have done with you. There is absolutely nothing you can do about what is happening now, nothing at all.

You will cry much because I am not going to let you give money to any of your children or your immediate family members now. You will have money but you will use it as I direct you to. They'll all be okay. They each have to learn the lesson the hard way just like you and the reason is they, like you, would not listen and wanted to do things their way. They will all soon realize it is My way or no way at all. The wages of sin is death but the gift of God is eternal life. There *is* a way that seems right to man but the end thereof is death. Those that I love, I chasten just like any good father.

Some are going to lose their physical lives because of their hardening of their hearts and disobedience, some in your family. But there will be many who will receive the blessings. It is not for you to know who will make it or who won't. That's only for Me to know.

I love you Regina and I am now fixing things so that no one will take advantage of you again. Be still and know that I am God. I've got this mess handled.

Last thing, I love you so much Regina. Well, Prophetess Regina Mixon, you have gotten your promotion."

Later God tells me not only is He about to bless my socks off but that He has been doing a breaking in The Word of God Church to build it up. He says He is now about to bless so many within that church and no devil in hell can stop what He is doing. He says we all can get ready to shake some haters off. Well, alright.

On Saturday, September 23rd, I met with Robert, a photographer, and discussed the book cover layout. It was a pretty interesting meeting but I walked away a bit discouraged. Prior to that I had mentioned to someone about my plans to be a motivational speaker, another male and again I became discouraged. Why did I lump these two together and why was I discouraged? Neither was really encouraging. That's some men for you.

However, with both men I did walk away with some really

great ideas. So, thanks as you helped me much anyway.

This book is targeted primarily for women. Men might find it too wordy. So, I'll get a woman to proof, edit and print this. God already had that in the plan. Pastor later supplied me with information on a publisher who just happens to be a woman, at least that's who I have constantly dealt with.

What time is it in my life? It's time to get my passport. It's time to finish this book. It's my time for my thing from my God. Hopefully, when you finish reading this, you too, will decide the same.

Sunday, October 22, 2006
Good morning God,

It's 8:20 AM and I just want to say good morning and thank You for waking me up this morning. Thank You God for watching over me and mine. Lord, I know I cannot be in every place watching over all of my family members but You can and I thank You. I am so grateful. I woke up this morning with home on my mind. After listening to a message on Trinity Broadcasting Network about fighting for one's family, my first thoughts were those of returning home. Being in California, I find myself alone so much. There is no closeness in the real sense. There has been a lot of division and a lot of confusion.

You know there have been many pluses which include having a great job, great co-workers, a great management team and super people to work with. This alone has made this journey bearable.

It seems sometimes when I try to reach out to others, the more I try, the harder it becomes. I'm thankful for each and every one of my neighbors. You know it goes without saying, I am so grateful for Dorothy, Jeffery and Shyeta. They seem to always make themselves available.

I am actually embarrassed by the situation here and often wonder how in the name of Jesus did this happen. The only answer I come up with is subtly. The enemy sneaked in because there was a crawl hole left for him to come in. Because of this, my life is not anywhere I had hoped and prayed it would be.

I've come to realize that many do have itching ears. There are so many that want to play church—hearing what they want to hear and living the way they want to live. Giving a person the word doesn't even seem to convict them.

I am not judging anyone as I know I have been there myself and am in no position to judge. Now I understand what my grandmother must have gone through. I understand it totally and completely. Nevertheless Lord, I know very little about anything. I just read, study, pray and listen to You. The only things I do know are those You share with me, both written and spoken.

Well God, I've poured my heart out to You. There is only one thing left and that is I fully understand the need for a Godly man as the head of this household now. By not having that, my life has actually been out of order for many years causing me and my children to suffer much. God, I am now ready for the person You have for me, one who accepts me for me and I, in return do the same with him.

Lord, I do love You and if You never, ever do anything else for me, that love will never change. You have already done so much for me and I am eternally grateful.

Your daughter,

Regina

His response—

"Regina, I know you love Me. You have proven it over and over again. The enemy has come at you in every way and you have stood. You've been lied on, cheated, talked about and mistreated, but through it all you have stood. I can trust you Regina. I can trust you to tell people what I say. I can trust you to do as I lead you to. It is over.

Your house is about to come in order real quick. No one, and I do mean no one, will hold up the blessings that I have for you. Not now, not ever. I've allowed you to go through hell. I knew from the very beginning that you would stand.

Regina, just like I speak to you I do speak to others. Many know that they have wronged you and yet insist on doing it their way. Watch what I do. Do NOT try to fight any battles. Allow Me to do it.

Regina, there is a male there that loves you very much. That person is hurting and so are you. This is not a game. You don't have to do anything but be still and watch Me move. I love you Regina and I always will and now I trust you to be very still. Watch some people change. Some of the things they said they wouldn't do, well, just watch My power.

Trust Me Regina. Just trust me. The book is ending. It is all coming to an end."

Somewhere during this period, God opened doors for the church to go to Trinity Broadcasting Network. It was an awesome experience. Out of no where (yeah right), I get a letter in the mail saying they were inviting me to be a part of the Trinity Broadcasting Network audience. After that took place contact was made with Joy Ferlauto with Trinity Broadcasting Network and the door was open to go many times and it still is an open door. Thank You God and thanks Joy. Awesome God!

My sister-in-law, Della, came to visit in early November. We had a ball. We visited her sister and nephew in Northern California and that's when things really started to change. It was at that point that I began to realize that we have lots of family here. I also came to realize that even though I had moved from home; my family and I are only a bus ride, plane or train ride, or car ride away from each other. After all, DI had made two trips out here, or was it three DI? Keisha and the kids had made three trips out here and now Della is here. I haven't lost my family. It seems I've just given them an opportunity to get a break and maybe have somewhere to go to visit. Thank You God!

    Della and I getting together can be really dangerous. Not really. But, we decided that we would, as a family, plan annual vacations to places we had not traveled to, making reservations well in advance and just have some fun. I know others have done this but we were all living in the same State together for a long time and had not. Slow, but still on target.

    At her sisters, in addition to faring sumptuously on the great fish that Lou cooked, we visited, shopped and the time just seemed to fly. Don't worry, we'll be back.

    Della's visit helped me to gather the strength that I needed to make some necessary changes. Two are most definitely better than one. There is so much power with two people walking together in agreement. I love you Della.

    She was so excited. Since I had no car and Nikki was in hers and gone, we rode the bus, Metro (train) and walked, all in one day. Before her visit was over she enjoyed a taxi ride in Los Angeles.

    You know that I just had to write many love letters after that to God. I thanked Him for things seen and unseen. I thanked Him so much. He knew just what I needed. I had felt so alone. I am not alone.

    God tells me later that He has a house in the plan for me and that I will live in it for a while and flip it later. He assures me that my daughter is going to get her act together. He said that she has to as He has great works for the both of us to do right here in California. He tells me that He has some great surprises for me. He says that I will never cry another tear of sadness again.

God tells me that Gail Marie Hughes King is my friend. He says that I have many others but Gail is a real friend that will stand by me through thick and thin. He told me that Gail is not one who will betray or desert me. He said for me to just trust Him and believe that. He told me that Gail is something good in my life. (I know this now)

God says to me that Gail is like me, that even though she is in the midst of lots of people, she desires that real friend. He said that she has some but He wants me to be that to her.

He goes on to tell me that DI is my friend but that I have so many others, so many He says. Annette Jones Davidson, God says, is a good friend as with all of those in Women of Purpose and Determination. (I believe that.)

You may wonder why God had to tell me who my friends are and that's valid. There had been several times in my life that I had been betrayed by people I considered friends, two instances immediately comes to mind. If God had not told me, even though others had continually tried to show me, I probably would have wandered and wondered for too long.

God says that He is about to change a person who is not a Christian to one suddenly. He says that He will take the foolish things of the world and confound the wise. I say He can do whatever He wants whenever He wants.

I write a letter to God on Sunday, November 12th, this just happens to have been my first child's birthday. I tell Him of my love. Well, here's a part of it——

"This vision You have given me is so much larger than Louisiana or Los Angeles even for that matter. It is so much bigger than one church; it is about the church—kingdom building.

It's about teaching, encouraging, edifying and helping…each other. Folks will readily accept any and everything I have to offer them but when I have asked for the help I need, all I have gotten is a lot of broken promises or no contact at all... silence. I don't even say to people "give", I say "invest". An investment yields a return. This is good ground as it's all about You. So, if it's to be it is up to You.

Once others realize that we were all handpicked and chosen to make a mark over the entire world and that by walking in obedience to You, we can impact many cities, states, and countries and start a revival of the Bible. When will some realize that there are people hungry (spiritually and physically) all over the world? Coming together we can have a greater impact that any one of us alone. You called *us* to do this. You called *us* to change a generation. You called *us*. Many are called but few are chosen. Those that You have placed in my path have all been chosen; at least that's my belief. We should all be ashamed.

You gave the vision. You put this burden in my heart for the people and I cannot remove this, only You can. I know You remember when You asked me the question several times, "Regina, lovest thou Me?" Then You said for me to feed Your sheep. Well, I am constantly working day and night, reading, studying, gathering information, making phone calls to get information to not only help myself but many, many others. They don't seem to want it."

Well, can God turn things around? Will God turn things around? Did God turn things around? Yes, to all three. We, being Gail King, Nikki and I, are in the process of getting R. E. G. S. Books, LLC established via all of the proper channels. The name has been obtained, the EIN and some other things necessary for business start ups. The bank account is being opened very soon.

R. E. G. S. Books, LLC will serve as a catalyst for aspiring writers to promote and market their books. I'll let some things be a surprise, don't want to give you too much information just yet. This is the first of many "for profit" businesses we will be a part of. Whoa! Didn't God say businesses would spring forth from "God's

Storehouse", successful ones at that? Well, I am looking at doing many as with Gail and Nikki. By the way, Shie, or rather Shyete Jean Mozeke, is another partner, she's just a silent partner for right now.

At The Word of God, there are some successful people there who are already teaching us about much needed areas in our lives. I think a marriage is about to take place. You thought I had forgotten, didn't you. Do you want to know who the lucky person is? Not yet.

Before I give you the answer to that one, allow me to answer one mentioned way back in this book. You know I said my mother told me years ago who my real dad was? Well that person is the person I affectionately have referred to as Pops. Some may get upset but I speak what I was told by not only her, but many others, and he did as well. The way I see it I was blessed with two dads and because of that have an extremely large family. I was not there at all when that happened.

One of the things that hurt so bad was the fact that when he went home to be with the Lord, only one person even acknowledged me outside of my family and Pastor Rodney Williams and his wife, Evangelist Cynthia Williams. That person was DI, the real one, Felonesecia West. Thank you so much Dee for the love shown.

To add something to this, my real Dad, the one who I really believe and know is my real Dad, is God Himself. Anyone else, well it really doesn't matter. God is the only Dad I will ever need. Well, my spiritual dad is about to change. Sorry Creflo.

Here comes the bride. Here comes the bride. There's a wedding taking place and you're all invited. This time it is not a wedding between the lady and a man nor is it a wedding between the lady and her Lord (that's already happened). This time the wedding that takes place is between none other than the lady and The Word of God MBC. You heard me right.

When does this event occur? Sunday, January 14, 2007. My brother's birthday is a most appropriate date.

After the hurts experienced, it took me all of these years to get to the healing and to be ready for this marriage. It took all of these years to be ready to fully commit to any church. I made it though and you're all invited. If you should happen to miss this date, have your own wedding. Get radical. Invite some people in. Put on your wedding dress and marry the Lord. He'll send your human lover in later but **He is** the lover of your soul. *She found herself.*

For those in the Los Angeles area that are looking for a church home, come and join us anytime. Come and get your praise on. We're right at the corner of forty eighth and Western in the city of Los Angeles. We have an awesome choir, praise dance ministry and many others to help meet the needs. You will be fed and leave full to the overflow. You can't miss us.

If you don't want to become a partner with us, go somewhere. There are many great churches in the area. Come one, come all. And remember, no matter when you come in or where you choose to call home, the pay will be the same in the eleventh hour as for those that came in the first hour. Don't wait too late. Procrastination robs you of too much. Later may be too late.

It is finished. ***"TO GOD BE THE GLORY!"*** Now I am ready.

Prayer for Salvation and Deliverance

Father God,

    I confess my sins to you today. I ask you to come into my life. I ask you Lord to forgive me of my sins. Your word says that if I confess my sins with my mouth and believe in my heart that Christ was raised from the dead, I would be saved. Today, I do both. Help me to walk the straight and narrow from this day forward. Give me the strength to say no to the things of this world and yes to you. Help me to realize that even in living the life before you that I will stumble and fall. Your word says a righteous man falls many times but he gets back up. Order my steps in Your word each and every day. Help me to be about Your business of encouraging, uplifting and assisting others all the days of my life. After all, it's ALL about You. Allow me to know that every day is a day of thanksgiving and not take anyone or anything for granted. Deliver me from the bondage that the enemy is trying to use to destroy me. I ask you to stop the attacks of the enemy in my life and those of my family members. Today I believe I am healed, delivered and set free; free to be the real me and free to do Your will. Thank you for not giving me a spirit of fear. Thank You for my soaring in life and being prosperous in every area of my life—spiritually, physically, relationally, and financially. Make me whole; blessed to be a blessing.

Today, I surrender my all to you.

In Jesus name and for his sake.

AMEN

www.ingramcontent.com/pod-product-compliance
Lightning Source LLC
Chambersburg PA
CBHW031246290426
44109CB00012B/464